The Shakespeare Handbooks

Richard III

Paul Prescott

First published 2006 by
PALGRAVE MACMILLAN
Houndmills, Basingstoke, Hampshire RG21 6XS and
175 Fifth Avenue, New York, N.Y. 10010
Companies and representatives throughout the world

PALGRAVE MACMILLAN is the global academic imprint of the Palgrave Macmillan division of St. Martin's Press, LLC and of Palgrave Macmillan Ltd. Macmillan® is a registered trademark in the United States, United Kingdom and other countries. Palgrave is a registered trademark in the European Union and other countries.

ISBN-13: 978–1–4039–4143–5 hardback
ISBN 10: 1–4039–4143–2   hardback
ISBN-13: 978–1–4039–4144–2 paperback
ISBN 10: 1–4039–4144–0   paperback

This book is printed on paper suitable for recycling and made from fully managed and sustained forest sources.

A catalogue record for this book is available from the British Library.

A catalog record for this book is available from the Library of Congress.

10   9   8   7   6   5   4   3   2   1
15   14   13   12   11   10   09   08   07   06

Printed in China

The Shakespeare Handbooks

THE SHAKESPEARE HANDBOOKS

Series Editor: John Russell Brown

PUBLISHED

FORTHCOMING

For Peter Prescott,
1936–2005

Contents

General Editor's Preface

The Shakespeare Handbooks provide an innovative way of studying the theatrical life of the plays. The commentaries, which are their core feature, enable a reader to envisage the words of a text unfurling in performance, involving actions and meanings not readily perceived except in rehearsal or performance. The aim is to present the plays in the environment for which they were written and to offer an experience as close as possible to an audience's progressive experience of a production.

While each book has the same range of contents, their authors have been encouraged to shape them according to their own critical and scholarly understanding and their first-hand experience of theatre practice. The various chapters are designed to complement the commentaries: the cultural context of each play is presented together with quotations from original sources; the authority of its text or texts is considered with what is known of the earliest performances; key performances and productions of its subsequent stage history are both described and compared. The aim in all this has been to help readers to develop their own informed and imaginative view of a play in ways that supplement the provision of standard editions and are more user-friendly than detailed stage histories or collections of criticism from diverse sources.

Further volumes are in preparation so that, within a few years, the Shakespeare Handbooks will be available for all the plays that are frequently performed and studied.

John Russell Brown

Preface

First, thanks are due to John Russell Brown for inviting me to contribute a Shakespeare Handbook. He has been a wise, patient and sympathetic general editor; I hope this offering does some justice to his original vision for the series.

Members of staff at the following libraries and archives have provided invaluable support: the National Theatre Archive, south London; the Theatre Museum, Covent Garden; the Shakespeare Centre, Stratford-upon-Avon; last but by no means least, thanks are due to Jim Shaw and Kate Welch of the Shakespeare Institute Library, Stratford-upon-Avon.

Although many friends and colleagues have helped to sustain or divert me during the writing of this book, direct thanks are due to the following: the members of the Shakespeare Institute MA option in *Richard III* in performance, way back in 2000, but especially Lauren Bergquist, Keith 'Chief' Condon, and Shirley Wright for their enduring friendships; Tom Lanoye and Luk Perceval for kindly allowing me to quote from *Ten Oorlog*, and Will (iloveshakespeare.com) Sutton for his post-haste translation of the extract; clever Neil Allan for Kafka; Paul Edmondson for steak and solidarity as we trod the same path; Kevin Crawford and all my friends at the Palm Beach Shakespeare Festival, Florida. Special gratitude is due to Greta von Unruh for being so lovable and, miraculously, so loving.

Four people braved earlier drafts of this book. Endurance awards to: Aaron Deveson, William Prescott, John Welch, and Stanley Wells. All four readers combine sharp eyes with a genius for generous encouragement for which I will always be grateful. All inaccuracies and infelicities remain my own.

I was eight years old when my home town celebrated (if that's the right word) the quincentenary of the little princes' sojourn in Stony Stratford (see II.iv.2). I am not sure whether I went to any of the events, but I still have the t-shirt somewhere. I have been lucky enough to spend significantly longer in Stony than the infant royals and this book is partly offered to the friends and family who have made, and continue to make, the stay such a rich pleasure. Thanks to the Deveson, Nevitt, Norgate, Pratt, Scrimshaw, and Welch families, and to my sisters, Anna and Maria. But final thanks, for their kindness and support (and for bringing us to Stratford-not-upon-Avon in the first place), are due to my parents, Philippa and William Prescott.

My uncle and godfather, Peter Prescott, died shortly before this book went to press. It is to the memory of this much-loved man – who was everything an uncle should be – that this book is dedicated.

A note on texts

All references to *Richard III* are keyed to John Jowett's 2000 Oxford edition of the play. It is not essential that readers have this by their side – any edition of the play will do. However, textual references will be more quickly traced, especially in the Commentary, if Jowett's edition is at hand. It also happens to be the best single-volume, scholarly edition of the play currently available. All quotes from other Shakespeare plays are taken from *The Complete Oxford Shakespeare* (second edition, 2005, edited by Stanley Wells, Gary Taylor, John Jowett and William Montgomery).

Paul Prescott

1 *The Texts and Early Performances*

Date of composition and first performance

In the early 1590s a theatrical legend was born. He had enjoyed a strong and increasingly intriguing supporting role in two earlier plays depicting the unhappy reign of King Henry VI and then, finally, was given his own star vehicle. In this new play, when he first limped on he needed no introduction. Perhaps the audience recognized the actor and his costume from the prequels; perhaps the uneven gait and misshapen body left no doubt as to his demonic persona. Throughout his long opening speech he felt no need to remind the spectators of his identity, and indeed, it was only in the 52nd line of the play, uttered by his brother Clarence, that they heard his name for the first time: Richard.

It is impossible to say with any certainty when exactly that historic entrance was made. The first performances of *Richard III* are not clearly recorded. Unlike most of Shakespeare's plays, it is not even certain which theatrical company employed the playwright at the time and thus premiered his new work. We know that Shakespeare acted with and wrote plays for the Lord Chamberlain's Men, founded in 1594. Before that, there is circumstantial evidence to link the young man-of-the-theatre with Lord Strange's Men, especially given the fact that the patron of the company, Ferdinando Lord Strange, was a descendant of the Lord Stanley whom Shakespeare treated – in contrast to his sources – so sympathetically in *Richard III*. However, this logic of association through flattery might equally link the play to the Earl of Pembroke's Men (formed 1592); late in the play, Shakespeare names Pembroke and

1

Sir Walter Herbert as rallying to support Richmond's cause
(IV.v.9–11). In the Folio text, Herbert is even on stage as a mute
companion to Richmond on the eve of the Battle of Bosworth. As
John Jowett speculates: 'Perhaps this attention to Herbert and
Pembroke was because Henry Herbert, second Earl of Pembroke,
was patron of the company now envisaged as about to perform
[*Richard III*]' (p. 6).

If the exact date of the first performance is impossible to establish, there are two key dates between which the premiere must have
taken place. On 20 September 1592, a pamphlet entitled *Greene's
Groatsworth of Wit* was entered in the Stationers' Register. The
author, satirizing the upstart crow Shakespeare, wrote of a 'Tiger's
heart wrapped in a player's hide', a clear parody of a line from
Richard Duke of York (I.iv.138 of what is more generally known as the
third part of *Henry VI*). That play is commonly dated to 1591 or early
1592, thus suggesting the latter year as the earliest possible date for
the composition and premiere of *Richard III*, which was obviously
intended as a conclusive sequel. Unfortunately, the next key date in
the play's early history occurs a full five years later, in 1597, with the
publication of the First Quarto (Q1), entitled *The Tragedy of King
Richard III*. 'Quarto' was the name given to a small-format, relatively
cheap text which was a quarter of the size of a standard printing
sheet. Before 1597, only two of Shakespeare's plays had been
published in quarto format: *Titus Andronicus* and *The First Part of the
Contention of the Two Famous Houses of York and Lancaster* (*2 Henry VI*)
both appeared in 1594; *The True Tragedy of Richard Duke of York and the
Good King Henry the Sixth* (*3 Henry VI*) was printed a year later in the
even smaller octavo format. All of these plays were published some
years after their first performances, and it is clear that a similar, if
not longer, gap occurred between the premiere of *Richard III* and its
appearance in print. On the balance of evidence, *Richard III* was
probably written sometime in 1592 and given its first performances
soon after, either on a provincial tour by Pembroke's Men, or in
London immediately before the closure of the theatres, owing to
plague, in June 1592, or quickly after their reopening in late
December that year.

The texts of *Richard III*

In 3 *Henry VI*, Richard of Gloucester soliloquizes on the many obstacles between him and the object of his desire, the crown. He imagines himself as

> one lost in a thorny wood,
> That rends the thorns and is rent with the thorns,
> Seeking a way and straying from the way,
> Not knowing how to find the open air
> But toiling desperately to find it out.

(III.ii.174–8)

A no less bewildering and disorienting obstacle-course confronts the editor of *Richard III*. For editors, the object of desire, the crown of their labours, is to produce a text for the modern reader that most nearly matches Shakespeare's intentions. *Richard III* exists in two substantive, and substantially different texts. The first version, already mentioned, is the Q1 text published in 1597. The second version was published twenty-six years later in the First Folio (F; 1623), in the 'Histories' section of the first 'complete works' of Shakespeare. In 1864, the editors of the Cambridge Shakespeare made the spine-chilling assertion: 'The respective origin and authority of the first Quarto and first Folio texts of *Richard III* is perhaps the most difficult question which presents itself to an editor of Shakespeare.' Decades of desperate toil on the part of editors to establish which of these texts more faithfully represents Shakespeare's play as it was performed in his lifetime have led to a range of theories and conclusions. A detailed survey of this complicated history is impossible here; readers are referred to the textual introductions and rationales of Hammond, Jowett and Taylor (see Further Reading, p. 172). Here at least we can survey some of the most telling differences between Q1 and F and consider their implications for performance.

No manuscript – in Shakespeare's or anyone else's handwriting – of *Richard III* exists. But it is clear that Q1 and F are the printed versions of substantially different manuscripts. F is about 200 lines longer than Q1 and there are literally hundreds of variants in both dialogue and stage directions between the two texts. The overwhelming question concerns the origins of these manuscripts. Q1 has typically been regarded as an inferior work to F; according to Antony Hammond, it is 'less regular metrically, less grammatically correct, often manifestly less verbally effective' (p. 3). This perceived inferiority led D. L. Patrick to conclude in his influential study *The Textual History of Richard III* (1936) that Q was a so-called 'bad' quarto, a text based not upon an authorial manuscript but upon memorial reconstruction. The theory runs that a company of actors, most probably while touring the play in the English provinces, found itself without a prompt book, and attempted to set down the play collectively from memory. In contrast with other 'bad' quartos (the first quarto of *Hamlet* being perhaps the most egregious example of faulty and amnesiac transmission) the actors did an excellent job of remembering the play, possibly because the playwright himself was in their midst. Whether in the Q or F version, *Richard III* is, after *Hamlet*, Shakespeare's second longest play. Perhaps to make it more stage-worthy, the acting version found in Q cuts 200 lines, but adds the highly theatrically effective 'clock' dialogue between Richard and Buckingham in Act IV, scene ii. Hundreds of other changes were introduced into the texture of the work: new synonyms, grammatical variations and changes in verb tenses and noun numbers riddled the resultant text.

Having battled through the thorny wood of editorial consideration, Hammond concluded his lengthy analysis of the claims of Q and F thus:

> The Quarto remains a document of primary importance in the textual history of *Richard III*, despite its ambiguous origins. Not only does it preserve evidence of the ways in which the play was adapted to performance by cutting and by book-keeper's alterations, but it also reveals, among its corruptions and mistakes, a layer of changes to the text which by any reasonable estimate must derive from Shakespeare.   (p. 20)

Despite the evidence of authorial revision in Q, Hammond nevertheless based his Arden edition on F. In the Oxford *Complete Works*, Gary Taylor also took F as his control text, whilst simultaneously acknowledging that Q was probably – despite the respective publication dates of Q and F – based on a later manuscript version of the play than F, a revised version that, for all its faults, is more theatrically attuned and performance-oriented than that of the Folio. Editing, like any other form of interpretation and publication, demands novelty, so it was perhaps a matter of time before the partial rehabilitation of Q resulted in it being used as the control text for an edition. Jowett's 2000 Oxford edition argued that the evidence for memorial reconstruction was 'far from compelling' (p. 124) and that the Q text is 'more plausibly designated "theatrical" than "memorial", and most of its theatricality seems intentional and constructive' (p. 127). In making Q1 the control text, 'a subtly different reading of the play' emerges:

> The emphasis is shifted away from a melodrama crowning a historical sequence sustained by a sense of fate and an appeal to pathos, towards a more secular, free-standing, and psycho-political drama about Richard's rise and fall in relation to a more narrowly prescribed group of other characters.   (p. 132)

Jowett's argument, like those of Hammond and Taylor before him, is ingenious and thorough. But unless some new piece of primary evidence is discovered, the debate is unlikely to be resolved once-and-for-all in either direction. A healthy agnosticism will be the best frame of mind for those future readers and editors 'seeking a way' to an ideal text of *Richard III*.

Original staging and success

Shakespeare's plays were written for immediate theatrical presentation. From 1594, when he joined and became a share-holder in the Lord Chamberlain's Men, he wrote for the specific architectural dynamics of a succession of playhouses: the Theatre, the Curtain, the Globe and, towards the end of his career, the new indoor theatre at Blackfriars. When he wrote *Richard III*, however, Shakespeare may not have been certain of exactly where his new play would be given its first staging. Flexibility was the key. As Andrew Gurr writes:

> The company might be summoned to play at court, at private houses, or at the halls of the Inns of Court as readily as at inns or innyards or the

custom-built theatres themselves. They travelled the country with their plays, using the great halls of country houses, or town guildhalls and local inns, wherever the town they visited allowed them.   (p. 3297)

On tour, many of the 'found spaces' of performance probably approximated to the basic configuration of the permanent theatres: a stage platform with entrances stage right and left; a trap-door in the floor; a pair of stage pillars; and, perhaps, a discovery space upstage centre, above it a gallery or upper level, and, more rarely still, above the playing area a 'heavens' with descent machinery. *Richard III* is dramaturgically straightforward: it requires no trap-door, no discovery space and no descent from the heavens. If some other solution is found for the moment when Richard appears '*between two bishops, aloft*' (III.vii.89.sd), it can even be performed on a single-level stage. The stage-world in which Richard bustled was uncluttered and unadorned. As is typical of Elizabethan theatre, words stand in for scenery. Location was established verbally: 'Welcome, sweet Prince, to London, to your chamber' (III.i.1); 'Stay, yet look back with me unto the Tower' (F IV.i.93) or more commonly left indeterminate. The use of stage properties was emblematic: the presence of a solitary throne would invite the audience to imagine the rest of the palace, to piece out the imperfection with their thoughts. With the exception of the two tents at Bosworth Field, the use of props and scenic items in *Richard III* borders on the frugal: a coffin (perhaps simply a stretcher of sorts) for the corpse of Henry VI, a prison bench for Clarence, a table for the council scene, a throne, an assortment of weapons, a bowl of wine, ink and various papers, and a light. With such an economy of staging needs, the play could, like its star, 'Change shapes with Proteus for advantages' (*3 Henry VI*, III.ii.192) and readily adapt itself to the dimensions of its host space.

Although much of the early history of the play is shrouded in mystery and open to speculation, one thing is clear: *Richard III* was popular. Popular with readers: the First Quarto was reprinted no fewer than four times during Shakespeare's own lifetime, apparently making it second only to *1 Henry IV* in terms of marketability. In 1614 a long poem by Christopher Brooke entitled 'The Ghost of Richard the Third' was published, which implies Shakespeare's play was still well known. In it, the shade of Gloucester addresses Shakespeare, his creator:

> To him that impt my fame with Clio's quill,
> Whose magick rais'd me from oblivion's den,
> That writ my storie on the Muses' hill,
> And with my actions dignifi'd his pen.

If the play was popular with readers and theatregoers, it was also a hit with actors, and with one actor in particular. In 1602, the diarist John Manningham recorded:

> Upon a time when Burbage played Richard III there was a citizen grew so far in liking him that before she went from the play she appointed him to come that night unto her by the name of Richard the Third. Shakespeare, overhearing their conclusion, went before, was entertained, and at his game ere Burbage came. Then message being brought that Richard the Third was at the door, Shakespeare caused return to be made that William the Conqueror was before the Richard the Third. Shakespeare's name [being] William.

Both playwright and actor were celebrities and their celebrity was intimately, even erotically, linked with the early performances and publications of *Richard III*.

2 *The Play's Sources and Cultural Contexts*

Richard in History

Shakespeare's use of his sources has been a major theme of much criticism of *Richard III* and the history plays in general (see Chapter 6, 'Critical Assessments'). Most of the debate centres on whether Shakespeare endorsed or implicitly critiqued the orthodox and Tudor-biased historical accounts of Richard's rise and reign on which he based his play. Of the five extracts printed below, the first three are direct sources for the play. They encapsulate the standard framework of historical interpretation within which Shakespeare wrote his play. It should be remembered (a) that it would have been impossible for Shakespeare's company to pass a play through the Master of the Revels' inspection that was explicitly critical of Henry Tudor (Richmond), Queen Elizabeth's grandfather, and (b) that all of the sources available to Shakespeare shared a common interpretation of history and character; the playwright would have looked in vain for a historian sympathetic to Richard, or a balanced account of his reign. Text 5 post-dates the composition of the play, but nevertheless reveals much about the social attitudes to deformity and disability held by many in Shakespeare's audience and, indeed, by Richard's enemies in the play.

1 *Sir Thomas More's 'The History of King Richard the Third'*

Shakespeare had more than a passing interest in the life and works of Sir Thomas More: sometime around 1603 he contributed passages to an earlier biographical play charting the Catholic martyr's life. *Sir*

Thomas More was probably originally written at about the same time that Shakespeare used More as a source for *Richard III*. More's engaging and partisan account of the rise to power of Richard III, as integrated into Raphael Holinshed's *Chronicles* of English history (1587 edition), provided Shakespeare with his main source for character, chronology and incident when writing much of *Richard III*. Holinshed's *Chronicles*, running to three folio volumes and approximately three and a half million words, was an abundant source for at least thirteen of Shakespeare's plays, as well as the source for more plays of the period than any other book (Jowett, p.12). More described Richard as 'little of stature, ill-featured of limbs, crook-backed, his left shoulder much higher than his right, hard-favoured of visage'. As if that wasn't bad enough, 'he was close and secret, a deep dissembler . . . arrogant of heart, outwardly companionable where he inwardly hated, not letting [omitting] to kiss whom he thought to kill'. There is also considerable overlap between More's persistently ironical authorial voice and the dramatic ironies which abound so freely in Shakespeare's play. The playwright's debt to the heavily biased historian is evident throughout the play until the moment of Buckingham's flight, at which point More ends his narrative. A good example of Shakespeare's close and creative adaptation of More's account can be found in the events surrounding the framing and subsequent execution of Hastings. The following short and edited extract from More should be read against the cross-referenced passages in the play.

On the Friday, being the 13th of June, many lords assembled in the Tower, and there sat in council, devising the honourable solemnity of the King's coronation. . . . These lords so sitting together communing of this matter, the Protector [Richard] came in amongst them, first about nine of the clock, saluting them courteously, and excusing himself that he had been from them so long, saying merrily that he had been a sleeper that day.

After a little talking with them, he said unto the Bishop of Ely, 'My lord, you have very good strawberries at your garden in Holborn. I require you let us have a mess of them.'   [see III.iv.1–38]

[Richard leaves the chamber]

And soon after one hour, between ten and eleven, he returned into the chamber amongst them all, changed, with a wonderful sour angry countenance, knitting his brows, frowning and fretting, and gnawing on his lips, and so sat him down in his place. . . . Then, when he had sat still a while, thus he began: 'What were they worthy to have that compass and imagine the destruction of me, being so near of blood unto the King, and Protector of his royal person and his realm?' At this question, all the lords sat sore astonished, musing much by whom this question should be meant, of which every man wished himself clear.

[Richard accuses the Queen of witchcraft]
Then said the Protector, 'Ye shall all see in what wise that sorceress and that other witch of her counsel, Shore's wife, with their affinity, have by their sorcery and witchcraft wasted my body.' And therewith he plucked up his doublet sleeve to his elbow upon his left arm, where he showed a wearish [shrivelled] withered arm, and small, as it was never other.

[All present suspect a plot, knowing that Richard's 'arm was ever such since his birth'. Hastings speaks first: 'Certainly, my lord, if they have so heinously done, they be worthy heinous punishment.']

'What,' quoth the Protector, 'thou servest me, I ween, with "if"'s and with "an"s. I tell thee, they have done so, and that I will make good on thy body, traitor.' And therewith, as in a great anger, he clapped his fist upon the board [table] a great rap, at which token one cried 'treason' outside the chamber. . . . Then were [the Lords] all quickly bestowed in diverse chambers, except the Lord Chamberlain [Hastings], whom the Protector bade speed and shrive him apace, 'For by St Paul,' quoth he, 'I will not to dinner till I see his head off.'   [see III.iv.64–84]

[Hastings is executed and Buckingham and Richard immediately falsify history.]
Now was this proclamation [of Hastings's treachery] made within two hours after that he was beheaded, and it was so curiously indited [carefully written] and so fair written in parchment, in so well a set hand, and therewith of itself so long a process, that every child might perceive that it was prepared before.   [see III.vi.1–14]

2   Edward Hall's 'The Union of the Two Noble and Illustre Families of Lancaster and York' (1548 and 1550)

A version of Hall's account was, like More's history, included in Holinshed's multi-authorial but interpretively consistent *Chronicles*. As noted above, More ends his history with Richard's accession to the throne. It was from other historians, then, that Shakespeare learned of the events between the coronation and Bosworth Field. The first blow dealt to Richard's authority as King is Buckingham's iciness and subsequent revolt. This is Hall's account of the break-up of the partnership.

> [Richard] so highly turned from him and so highly conspired against him, that a man would marvel whereof the change grew in so short space. Some say that the occasion was that a little before the coronation [after the coronation, in Shakespeare], the Duke required the king amongst other things to be restored to the Earl of Hertford's lands. . . . King Richard . . . rejected the Duke's request, with many spiteful and minatory [threatening] words, which so wounded the Duke's heart with hatred and mistrust, that he could never after endure to look right on King Richard but ever feared [for] his own life. 'For when I myself [said Buckingham] sued to him for my part of the Earl of Hereford's lands which his brother King Edward wrongfully detained and withheld from me . . . he did not only first delay me, and afterward deny me, but gave me such unkind words, with such taunts . . . as though I had never furthered him but [had] hindered him, as though I had put him down and not set him up: yet all these ingratitudes and undeserved unkindness I bore closely and suffered patiently and covertly remembered. . . . But when I was credibly informed of the death of the young innocents, his own natural nephews, contrary to his faith and promise – to the which, God be my judge, I never agreed nor condescended [agreed to] – O lord, how my veins panted, how my body trembled, and my heart inwardly grudged, in so much that I so abhorred the sight and much more the company of him, that I could no longer abide in his court, except [unless] I should be openly revenged. The end [likelihood of success] whereof was doubtful, and so I feigned a cause to depart, and with a merry countenance and a spiteful heart I took my leave humbly of him (he thinking nothing less than that I was displeased) and so returned to Brecknock. [see IV.ii.1–31, 84–124]

3 'The Mirror for Magistrates' (1559 and later editions)

The Mirror for Magistrates collected the work of a variety of poets on the theme of the rise and fall of great individuals in English history. Like Shakespeare, the authors drew on Hall (and in later editions, Holinshed) to create poetry. Perhaps unlike Shakespeare, their intention was clearly didactic and moral. Shakespeare made particular use of the 'tragedies' (as each poem is called) of Clarence, Hastings, and Shore's Wife, and was familiar with, if not as influenced by, those of

Edward IV, Rivers, Buckingham and Richard himself. In William Baldwin's poem, this is how Clarence, speaking from beyond the grave, recounts his death. After one of his servants was executed for necromancy, Clarence quarrelled with the King . . .

> For this I was commanded to the Tower,
> The King my brother was so cruel hearted:
> And when my brother Richard saw the hour
> Was come, for which his heart so sore had smarted,
> He thought best take the time before it parted.
> For he endeavoured to attain the crown,
> From which my life must needs have held him down.
>
> For though the King within a while had died,
> As needs he must, he surfeited so oft,
> I must have had his children in my guide
> So Richard should beside the crown have cost:
> This made him ply the while the wax was soft,
> To find a mean to bring me to an end,
> For realm-rape spareth neither kin nor friend.
>
> And when he saw how reason can assuage
> Through length of time, my brother Edward's ire,
> With forged tales he set him new in rage,
> Till at the last they did my death conspire.
> And though my truth sore troubled their desire,
> For all the world did know mine innocence,
> Yet they agreed to charge me with offence.
>
> This feat achieved, yet could they not for shame
> Cause me be killed by any common way,
> But like a wolf the tyrant Richard came,
> (My brother, nay 'my butcher' I may say)
> Unto the Tower, when all men were away,
> Save such as were provided for the feat:
> Who in this wise did strangely me entreat.
>
> His purpose was, with a prepared string
> To strangle me, but I bestirred me so,
> That by no force they could me thereto bring,
> Which caused him that purpose to forego.

> Howbeit they bound me whether I would or no,
> And in a butt of Malmsey standing by,
> New Christened me, because [so that] I should not cry.

4　*Elizabeth's coronation and the Tudor Myth (1559)*

On Saturday, 14 January 1559, the day before her coronation, Princess Elizabeth processed from the Tower towards Westminster. At Gracechurch Street she witnessed a pageant, performed by children, which depicted the union of Henry VII and Elizabeth, and drew optimistic and predictably sycophantic parallels between the two Elizabeths. The following verses of explication were spoken by a child to the imminent sovereign. Each stanza referred, in ascending order, to a level of a three-tiered structure; each platform contained symbolic representations of the named subjects. Here, at the beginning of Elizabeth's reign, is the unadulterated Tudor Myth.

> The two Princes that under one cloth of state,
> 　The man in the red rose, the woman in the white,
> Henry VII, and Queen Elizabeth his mate,
> 　By ring of marriage as man and wife unite.
>
> Both heirs to both their bloods, to Lancaster the King,
> 　The Queen to York, in one the two houses did knit;
> Of whom as heir to both, Henry the Eighth did spring,
> 　In whose seat, his true heir, Queen Elizabeth doth sit.
>
> Therefore as civil war, and feud of blood did cease
> 　When these two houses were united into one,
> So now that jars shall stint, and quietness increase,
> 　We trust, O noble Queen, thou wilt be cause alone.

5　*Francis Bacon, 'Of Deformity'*

Although written and first published (1612) roughly twenty years after Shakespeare wrote *Richard III*, Bacon's short essay offers an insight into orthodox attitudes to disability and deformity in early modern England. Although Bacon seems to acknowledge that a

deformed body does not inevitably signify a deformed mind, deformity is seen as an almost invariable determinant of personality. The
'perpetual spur' and 'industry' are neat analogues for Richard's energetic 'bustle'. It is not impossible that Shakespeare's play, with its
portrait of the rise of a great wit while his enemies sleep, influenced
Bacon's essay.

> Deformed persons are commonly even with [revenged on] nature; for as
> your nature hath done ill by them, so do they by nature; being for the
> most part (as the Scripture saith) 'void of natural affection'; and so they
> have their revenge of nature. Certainly there is a consent between the
> body and the mind; and where nature erreth in the one, she ventureth
> [risks failure] in the other. But ... the stars of natural inclination are
> sometimes obscured by the sun of discipline [education] and virtue.
> Therefore it is good to consider of deformity, not as a sign, which is more
> deceivable [untrustworthy]; but as a cause, which seldom faileth of the
> effect.
>   Whosoever hath any thing fixed in his person that doth induce
> contempt, hath also a perpetual spur in himself to rescue and deliver
> himself from scorn. Therefore all deformed persons are extreme bold.
> First, as in their own defence, as being exposed to scorn; but in process of
> time by a general habit. Also it stirreth in them industry, and especially of
> this kind, to watch and observe the weakness of others, that they may
> have somewhat to repay [revenge]. Again, in their superiors, it quencheth
> jealousy towards them, as persons that they think they may at pleasure
> despise: and it layeth their competitors and emulators asleep; as never
> believing they should be in possibility of advancement, till they see them
> in possession [of a position of power]. So that upon the matter, in a great
> wit, deformity is an advantage to rising.

The Dramatic Context of *Richard III*

The success and achievement of *Richard III* depended on a startlingly
original synthesis of a range of literary and dramatic precedents. In
turning history into theatre, Shakespeare hybridized elements of
classical, medieval and contemporary drama. Theatregoers had
already seen plays inspired by the classical revenge tragedies of
Seneca, had revelled in Machiavellian vice figures, had discerned the

deep structure of the morality play undergirding the modern drama, had even beheld Richard himself strutting and fretting his hour upon the stage. But to see and hear these ingredients for the first time so richly and harmoniously combined in one afternoon of theatregoing must have been dazzling.

Shakespeare was probably about twenty-eight when he wrote *Richard III*. Over half his life was already behind him. In front of him, stretched like so many undiscovered countries, the thirty plays and the two decades in which he would write more intensively and creatively than any human being before or since. According to Harold Bloom, he would go on to invent nothing less than our modern understanding of what it is to be human. But when the man in his late twenties wrote *Richard III*, it can be said, less controversially, that he was in the process of inventing the history play. All chronologies of Shakespeare's early career are more or less speculative, but following that established by the Oxford edition, it is probable that Shakespeare had written six plays when he turned to *Richard*: two comedies (*The Two Gentlemen of Verona*, *The Taming of the Shrew*), one tragedy (*Titus Andronicus*), and the trilogy of plays dealing with the reign of Henry VI. 'History plays' is not necessarily how Shakespeare or any of his audience would have described the three parts of *Henry VI*. In a real sense, the genre comes into being as a critical term only with the publication, thirty years later, of the First Folio, in which Shakespeare's works were editorially divided into the enduring classifications of 'Comedies', 'Histories' and 'Tragedies'. When first published as quartos, five of the seven plays we now call 'histories', including *Richard III*, were described as tragedies on their title pages.

The comedies demonstrated, amongst other things, an incipient fascination with role-playing, and the comparison between life and theatre that would preoccupy the playwright throughout his career. In what was probably his first play, *The Two Gentlemen of Verona*, Shakespeare named one of those gentlemen Proteus and invested in him the actorly qualities of shape-shifting, deceit and a sense of danger. *The Taming of the Shrew* goes much further down the meta-theatrical path: it begins with an induction in which the sloshed Christopher Sly is tricked into believing himself to be a Lord. The story of Kate and Petruchio – a 'kind of history' (Induction 2, line 135) as Bartholomew puts it, reminding us of the elasticity of the word – is a play-within-the-play put on for his benefit. Although Shakespeare does not return to the frame (as the possible source play, *The Taming of A Shrew*, did), it is clear that he asked his audience to treat the main story as a theatrical construct; in Prospero's famous image, 'an insubstantial pageant' on the cusp of truth and fiction. Such self-conscious theatricality is everywhere evident in *Richard III*, most notably in the thespian exchange between Richard and Buckingham before the faked *coup d'état* in Act III, scene v.

Of more obvious and immediate inspiration for the themes and dramaturgy of *Richard III* was the series of plays in which Shakespeare depicted the internecine decline of England following the death of Henry V. These epic, episodic plays rollercoast their way through the bitter conflict of the houses of York and Lancaster. Chivalry and heroism (as exemplified by such characters as Talbot, Bedford and Gloucester) are rapidly vanishing qualities, and the pursuit of power becomes an end itself. There is no action on stage in *Richard* as sadistic or shocking as Margaret's taunting of York with paper crown and bloodied handkerchief in *3 Henry VI* (Act I, scene iv, and remembered in *Richard III* at I.iii.171ff.), although the limb-chopping, child-eating carnage of *Titus Andronicus*, written soon after, implies that York got off lightly. The *Henry VI* plays portray a noisy, brutal and degenerative world, an abattoir in which right is usurped by might. And audiences – apparently – loved them. The introduction of Richard's ambition for the crown, combined with the uneasy optimism of Edward's closing line ('For here, I hope, begins our lasting joy', *3 Henry VI*, V.vii.46), strongly suggest that *Richard* was already fermenting in the playwright's mind and that a conclusive sequel was inevitable.

Richard before Shakespeare

Shakespeare was not the first playwright to exploit the dramatic potential of the infamous crookbacked King. Around 1579, a Cambridge academic, Thomas Legge, wrote *Ricardus Tertius*, a Latin version of Richard's story which Shakespeare probably never saw or read. What distant similarities there are between Legge's and

Shakespeare's plays can perhaps be attributed to the common influence of Seneca and their shared historical sources. The case is different with *The True Tragedy of Richard III*, acted by the Queen's Men and anonymously published in 1594. The direction of influence is complicated by dates, as it is impossible to state confidently which play was written first. In *The True Tragedy* we hear the lines:

> King.   A horse, a horse, a fresh horse.
> Page.   Fly, my Lord, and save your life!
> King.   Fly, villain? Look I as though I would fly?

> (ll. 1985–7)

In Hall's historical account of Bosworth, no request for a horse is made and the moment is hardly accentuated. Did Shakespeare hear for the first time the dramatic potential for what was to become one of his most iconic lines at a performance of the *True Tragedy*? Or had he already made the line so notorious that another playwright could not fail to echo it? Shakespeare had a knack of transforming the Queen's Men's plays (such as their version of *King John*) and replacing their orthodox literalism with dynamic complexity. If the *True Tragedy* does indeed pre-date Shakespeare's play, it is interesting that the influence is largely negative: in effect, the *True Tragedy* showed Shakespeare how *not* to write about Richard. Roughly one-sixth of the earlier play elapses before the protagonist even sets foot on stage, whereas Shakespeare, of course, could not wait to show off his star. The *True Tragedy* opens with a nod to Thomas Kyd's *The Spanish Tragedy*: the Ghost of Clarence initiates the play with a call for revenge. It then not only delays Richard's entrance, but also dwells on a number of events from the *Chronicles* – such as the humbling of Jane Shore – which failed to interest Shakespeare. If Shakespeare did indeed set himself the task of improving an earlier play beyond recognition, he was honing a creative method which would later lead to such pinnacles of his art as *Hamlet* and *King Lear*.

Seneca, Kyd and Marlowe

In 1581, Thomas Newton published *Seneca His Tenne Tragedies*, a translation by diverse authors of the Roman playwright's extant texts into

English. Whether Shakespeare knew them mainly in the original
Latin or through these new translations, it is clear that Seneca's
tragedies influenced the composition of *Richard III*. It is notable, for
example, that at moments when his historical sources are thin or
non-existent – moments like the wooing of Anne, Clarence's dream,
or the women's lamentation (IV.iv.4) – Shakespeare seems to look to
Seneca for dramatic inspiration. Harold F. Brooks has shown how
the attempt to seduce Anne replays the similarly outrageous task
Lycus sets himself with Megara in *Hercules Furens*; how Clarence's
dream draws heavily on a Senecan word-and-image base; and how,
in the scene of communal grief, Shakespeare's women resemble the
war-battered Hecuba, Helen and Andromache of the *Troades*. Other
Senecan features include the use of a prologue-like opening monologue, the choric role performed by Margaret, the highly structured
use of oratory, the characteristic bouts of stichomythia, and the more
generalized sense of a royal house labouring under a curse which
only bloodshed can expiate.

The contemporary play most influenced by Seneca, and the piece
which in turn perhaps most deeply influenced *Richard III*, was
Thomas Kyd's phenomenal *The Spanish Tragedy*. Written sometime
between 1585 and 1587, and published at least as early as 1592, Kyd's
play has been described as the first extant modern tragedy and 'quite
the most important single play in the history of English drama'
(McAlindon, p. 55). Directly influenced by both the techniques and
the ethos of Senecan tragedy, Kyd's plot plays itself out in an atmosphere thick with evil and stewed in corruption. Revenge and retribution are widely sought: Don Andrea, whose ghost watches the action
as it unfolds, seeks vengeance on Balthazar for his death in battle;
Bel-imperia, Don Andrea's lover, seeks, too, to revenge him;
Balthazar and Lorenzo murder Horatio for winning Bel-imperia's
love; and, most movingly, Horatio's father Hieronimo pursues
vengeance for his son's murder. All this is framed by the onstage
audience of Don Andrea's Ghost and the allegorical figure of
Revenge, who has, as it were, already read the script: the apocalypse
of inventively vivid deaths and dismemberments that ensues is
predetermined and unassailable. The sense of characters being
trapped in an overarching design of catastrophe, and the levels of

irony consequent from their ignorance of the true situation, is an innovation that inspired Shakespeare throughout *Richard III*. Although verbal correspondences between the two plays are few, Shakespeare learnt much from this Englished Senecanism. Margaret's function of keeping the memory of the past alive in the present echoes Hieronimo's obsessive refusal to forget; the Virgilian underworld described in Clarence's dream is foreshadowed in Andrea's prologue ('I saw more sights than thousand tongues can tell', I.i..57); and, in the following stichomythic exchange between Bel-imperia and Horatio (with sinister interjections from their onstage audience), we can hear the crisp repetitions and inversions of Richard's twin wooing scenes, of the ironic asides of the uncle with his nephews, and of Margaret's eavesdropping on the court:

> BEL-IMPERIA   But whereon dost thou chiefly meditate?
> HORATIO   On dangers past, and pleasures to ensue.
> BALTHAZAR   On pleasures past, and dangers to ensue.
> BEL-IMPERIA   What dangers and what pleasures dost thou mean?
> HORATIO   Dangers of war and pleasures of love.
> LORENZO   Dangers of death, but pleasures none at all.
>
> (II.ii.26–31)

Whilst Kyd's play decisively inflected the atmosphere in which Shakespeare steeped the self-destructive convulsions of the House of York, it did not offer a model on which to base Richard. For that inspiration, Shakespeare would have to look elsewhere.

In *3 Henry VI*, the younger Richard attempts to reinvigorate his father's campaign for the throne: 'father, do but think / How sweet a thing it is to wear a crown, / Within whose circuit is Elysium / And all that poets feign of bliss and joy' (I.ii.28–31). Hearing that, Shakespeare's audience must have thrilled to the rapture of ambition; it was a rapture they had heard before in the lines of Christopher Marlowe. In the years preceding his murder in May 1593, Marlowe's extravagant and erring spirit blazed its trail across the English stage. For the great actor Edward Alleyn, and the theatre company the Admiral's Men, he wrote a succession of remarkable roles. Faustus, Barabas (*The Jew of Malta*), Tamburlaine, and the Duke of Guise (*The Massacre at Paris*) brought an unprecedented energy, drive and restlessness to their dramas. Guise, the architect of the St Bartholomew's Day Massacre, boasts in a self-revealing soliloquy: 'That like I best that flies beyond my reach' (I.ii.41). This glamour of unending ambition spurs Marlowe's heroes to flout moral and social codes in their pursuit of the unachievable. Although we do not know for which company Shakespeare wrote *Richard III*, it would clearly have been in competition with the Admiral's Men at the Rose Theatre. Shakespeare's challenge was to write a role for Richard Burbage that could bear comparison with, if not out-face, the inflated virtuosi served up by Marlowe for Alleyn.

Of all Marlowe's plays, *The Jew of Malta* (*c*.1590) offered Shakespeare a first-class example of how to make murder funny and immorality entertaining. Richard's promise to 'set the murderous Machiavel to school' (*3 Henry VI*, III.ii.193), as well as being a generalized invocation of the depraved skulduggery associated with the Italian, was also a more specific reminder of the 'Machevill' who delivers the prologue to *The Jew of Malta*. With lip-smacking relish, he told his audience: 'I count religion but a foolish toy, / And hold there is no sin but ignorance' (Prologue, 14–5); Richard, in a similar vein, claims 'Conscience is but a word that cowards use, / Devised at first to keep the strong in awe' (*Richard III*, V.vi.38–9). Marlowe's characterization of Barabas, the eponymous Jew, influenced the genesis of Richard. Both are outsiders, an eccentricity that might have been physically marked on the Elizabethan stage by the wearing of a red wig and beard or, in Richard's case, some manner of hump. Both are determined to exploit and destroy the mediocrities that surround them, those common men, as Barabas puts it 'that measure naught but by the present time'. Minds like his (and Richard's), in contrast, are always aggressively pushing towards the future: 'A reaching thought will search his deepest wits, / And cast with cunning for the time to come' (I.ii.224–6). Barabas's lust for wealth, like Richard's for the crown, leads him to commit many atrocities, but, as in Shakespeare, this villainy is complicated by his collusive relationship with the audience and his comic bravura. Marlowe's fusion of influences from classical and native medieval drama was exemplary. Tamburlaine descended both from Seneca's Hercules Oetaeus and from the Herods and Pilates, the out-sized, scenery-chewing villains of the medieval Mystery Plays. Tamburlaine repeatedly describes himself as 'the Scourge of God', making explicit an identity that Shakespeare keeps implicit throughout as a point of reference for Richard.

Just as Richard explicitly flags his family resemblance to Marlowe's villains through his reference to Machiavelli, so he also reminds the audience of another dramatic source when, while deceiving the Prince, he turns to us with the aside:

> Thus like the formal Vice Iniquity
> I moralize two meanings in one word.

> (III.i.82–3)

The Vice was a stock character in medieval and Tudor morality plays, an emissary from Satan sent to tempt a no less allegorical representative of humankind. Richard's Vice-like qualities include his use of asides and his glee in sharing his plans with the audience, his satirical and anarchic edge, his power-lust, his outlandish appearance, his flippant amorality, and his knack of seductive persuasion. The medieval roots of *Richard III* can be glimpsed, for example, in one of forty-eight medieval mini-dramas that constitute the York Pageant play cycle. In 'The Fall of Man', the action begins with Satan on stage alone, airing his grievances to us and sharing his plan to be revenged on God. In the scene that follows, we see him putting this into effect and seducing Eve into eating the forbidden fruit in the Garden of Eden. It is not hard to see the same dramatic DNA at work in Richard's opening soliloquy and the subsequent conquest of Anne.

The influence of the morality play's characteristic Manichean structure, in which a Good and Bad angel fight over the soul of the protagonist, has even led some critics to suggest that this holds the key to the play's meaning. Irving Ribner, for example, argues: 'England [is] a kind of morality hero torn between good and evil forces; in *Richard III* she suffers the depths of degradation, and finally through God's grace she is allowed to win salvation by proper choice: the acceptance of Henry Richmond as king' (p. 114). This overstates the case. As we have seen, the range of influences that informed

Shakespeare's act of creation cannot be reduced to such a straightforward image. *Richard III* gains much of its buoyant theatricality
from heterogeneity. It unleashes a Marlovian hero on a Senecan
world and lets loose a chirpy Vice in the darkened chambers of
tragedy. It was an audacious synthesis and one that produced
Shakespeare's first masterpiece.

3 Commentary

Prologue

There is a moment before most theatrical performances when the audience decides for itself that the event is about to begin. The volume of chatter dissolves to near silence and the separate individuals who have made the trip to the theatre become unified as a body of spectators. For the first time the audience acts collectively. Before every performance of *Richard III* it is probable that this moment is heavy with expectation: somewhere backstage he is waiting to step forward and deliver himself to our eyes and ears. Over the following pages, I want to offer a detailed commentary on what might happen next. The cleanliness and predictable regularity of printed texts – all margins aligned, all font the same size, long speeches with the appearance of forbidding monuments – all this can, if we are not careful, lull us into reading Shakespeare's plays as epic poems, or, more broadly, as Literature. Nor is there anything wrong with this. The artefact belongs to us, its audience, and it is our individual right to enjoy and value it on whatever level we choose. But if (cf. Chapter 6, Critical Assessments) we cannot be sure what Shakespeare intended this piece to mean, we can at least be sure that he meant it to be performed. That is, our enjoyment and valuation of the text is liable to increase if we can either see it in performance, or, while reading, make the effort to imagine the words as spoken in concrete situations by actors who are aware of our presence and are seeking to thrill, excite and move us.

This commentary, then, is designed as an aid to help readers theatricalize their experience of the text. It will move through the play from moment to moment and scene to scene describing the variety of challenges and decisions faced in translating the play from two to three dimensions. This is not an account of how I personally would direct the play – that aim would be better achieved by actually staging it. Rather, this commentary is interested in possibilities, not prescription. Words such as 'might', 'perhaps', 'could', 'imply' and other bet-hedgers therefore occur frequently. As far as possible, the simultaneous possibility of alternative interpretations is stressed. Even so, it would be impossible to exhaust, in print, the range of gestures, inflections, expressions, character readings and stage compositions that might be inspired by this text. But by stressing at least some of the performance options, it will enable readers to create others for themselves.

I have assumed that the reader will visualize the action as taking place on a traditional, proscenium-arch-style stage. Occasional refer-ences to upstage and downstage will make sense in this context, although there is nothing to stop the reader imagining the action in any number of theatrical spaces, whether in the round, in traverse, on a thrust stage, in a park, or in a 'found' space of any description. Many of the interpretative challenges remain the same. One of these concerns cutting the text. Logistical and economical constraints – last trains, last orders, overtime for stage crews, the inconvenience of child actors and large casts, the discomfort of most theatre seating, etc. – generally make an uncut text unpopular with artists and audi-ences alike. This commentary nevertheless describes the action as it would, or does, unfold in a full-text performance. Whilst some passages are obvious candidates for cutting or pruning, I will not point them out: it is up to the reader–director to decide which moments seem redundant or simply expendable given the emphasis of their interpretation of the play.

In a text such as *Richard III* that is so densely populated with char-acters, it is sometimes difficult for the reader to make the effort to distinguish between speakers or to keep the non-speakers in mind as stage presences. I have tried to flag the silences of non-speakers, as well as placing characters' names in **bold** at the point of their first entrance, a pale typographical imitation of the interest aroused by our first encounter with a stranger. All references are to John Jowett's Oxford edition of the play.

ACT I

Act I, scene i

Entry   The stage is empty. Do the house lights in the auditorium dim, or plunge us into darkness? How long are we left there, between two worlds, before the stage is illuminated? When light hits the playing space, is he there, waiting for us? Or is the expectation tautened – do we have to wait for him? Is the entrance instantaneous or protracted? How much do we see his body in motion? How laborious is movement for him? Such questions will be settled in a matter of seconds. However the man gets to us – for he needs us as much as we want him – there is no denying the elemental power of his position. Before he entered, our spectatorship was unfettered, free to glance and flit. Now all eyes are focused on one body, an irresistible centripetal force impelling every gaze in the theatre. Had two or more bodies entered the stage, we would have some choice in locating our attention. Here there is no choice. He acknowledges our presence. He has something to tell us. 'Now is the winter of our discontent . . .'.

1–13   One of Shakespeare's most famous soliloquies is actually a straightforward affair in terms of the burden of conveying information and attitude. The opening line, while almost oppressively familiar, is nowhere near as nerve-racking for actor and audience as 'To be or not to be', in which actors often strain to new mint their phrasing. 'Now is the winter of our discontent' makes no sense without its sequel lines, and the energy supplied by the enjambment carries the actor through to the speech's first resting point, 'buried' (l. 4). The further repetitions of 'now' in lines 5 and 10 help to structure the opening movement of the soliloquy and sustain the sense of immediacy. (Shakespeare also began *A Midsummer Night's Dream* with this most theatrical of monosyllables.) If the opening 13 lines are straightforward, and the thumbnail sketch of the courtier (perhaps King Edward) capering to a lute is designed to warm the audience to Richard's satirical vision, the second movement ('But I . . .', ll. 14ff.) demands that the actor make some decisions with far-reaching consequences.

How much of Richard's body have we seen so far? The opening soliloquy is a strip-tease of sorts, in which Richard peels off the layers that clothe his naked villainy and reveals to us his evil. As with a stripper, the purpose is to titillate, but perhaps even more analogously, we, the audience, are fascinated by the body of the performer. Richard's entrance will, of course, draw attention to the extent of the character's deformity – although it may also mask it – but here, in the speech, the actor must not only show his disability, but also reveal his attitude towards it. Is he distanced from his suffering through familiarity? Does he feel contempt for his body or is he comfortable with it? Perhaps of overwhelming importance for the actor is the exact nature of the deformity. Through what ensues, we will hear Richard described as, among other unappealing things, a 'bunch-backed toad' (I.iii.246), 'bottled spider' (I.iii.242), 'hedgehog' (I.ii.100), and 'abortive rooting-hog' (I.iii.225) and we will hear him refer to his own arm as a 'blasted sapling withered up' (III.iv.74). These might be used as clues to his physical appearance. Equally, though, the animalistic references can't all be taken as literal descriptions, or Richard would look like a walking menagerie or a one-man zoo. Likewise, Richard's reference to his arm might be unreliable, a hoax to trap Hastings. A line not frequently referenced in relation to Richard's deformity can be found in *3 Henry VI* when Richard tells Clifford: 'Suppose this arm is for the Duke of York, / And this for Rutland, both bound to revenge' (II.iv.2–3), from which one can only assume both arms are *capable* of revenge. He clearly must limp – dogs bark at him as he 'halts' by them (l. 23) – but the severity of that limp is up to the actor, who may have to sustain the imbalance over the course of four hours. He is badly shaped, ill-proportioned, cheated of 'feature', a word which could mean both a good body and an attractive face. These self-descriptions, whilst consistent with each other, are not explicit or in any sense medically descriptive. Working only within the very broad parameters of what is considered physically unattractive, the actor is free to sculpt his face and body into any number of combinations.

14–27 This passage of the opening soliloquy demands that Richard both use his body to illustrate the description of his deformity, whilst also suggesting an attitude towards that deformity. The succeeding section logically begins with 'And therefore . . .' (l. 28) and ushers us towards the play's action. How convincing is the neat opposition of 'since I cannot prove a lover . . . I am determinèd to prove a villain' (ll. 28–30)? In the context of the tetralogy, we might think back to his claim that 'love forswore [i.e. abandoned] me in my mother's womb' (*3 Henry VI*, III.ii.153), a far stronger motivational source for the homicidal spree on which he is about to embark than the notion that his villainy springs from the inability to woo and have sex with women. The actor might note that Richard's mother will later, after wishing she had strangled him in her womb (IV.iv.132), describe his birth as a 'grievous burden' (IV.iv.160). Her pain, caused it is implied by his already misshapen body, has contributed to her withholding of love from the infant and the man. Thus, when Richard speaks of not being a lover, a long history of not being loved, of unlovability, is compacted into the expression. And the primal cause for that lack is his body.

28–116 Having inducted us to a peaceful, sportive court and to Richard's outsider status within it, the drama for the first time looks forward. The seeds for much of the action of the first Act are sown: King Edward and Clarence must be set in 'deadly hate the one against the other' (l. 35). As if by conjuration, **Clarence** enters, accompanied by **Brackenbury** and under '*a guard of men*', a permissive stage direction that could mean he's gently escorted by two 'armed' but sympathetic civil servants or roughly bundled across the stage by twenty heavily armed soldiers: this will depend on what type of political state the director is seeking to evoke and what kind of threat Clarence is perceived to pose to Edward's children. When Clarence refers to the Tower it is the first time in the play that a sense of location has been superimposed on the scene: we now know that on one side of the stage lies imprisonment, and that the other direction instantaneously assumes the symbolic value of liberty. Richard works the 'open air' (l. 124) space between freedom and incarceration like a burlesque Charon the ferryman. It is tempting to reverse-engineer Clarence's personality, assuming because he has a highly poetical set piece later in the play (in Act I, scene iv) that he is always a sensitive soul with a beautiful voice. This overlooks the 'lusty George' (*3 Henry*

VI, I.iv.75) and the somewhat shifty, side-swapping pragmatist of the former play.

This is Richard's first opportunity to entertain us at someone else's expense and he spends freely, combining faux naivety, catty misogyny and a harried persecution complex in his effort to persuade Clarence that Mistress Shore, the Queen and her kindred are responsible for his arrest (ll. 63–9). As the two brothers talk, their conversation becomes more intimate, hinting that they physically isolate themselves from the guards and Brackenbury, who is finally forced to interrupt (ll. 84–7). Richard responds with a sanitized version of their conversation, performed with a wink to Clarence, who (like us) feels pleased to be let in on Richard's irony. The chameleon then changes colours again from the bawdy surrounding Mistress Shore to the tear-stained hug he gives Clarence before he is led off to the Tower (see I.iv.224–6 for Clarence's retrospective account of this moment).

117–43 Briefly, the stage is Richard's again for a quick flash of conspiracy, then **Hastings** enters as if from the Tower. Hastings, 'the King's chiefest friend' (*3 Henry VI*, IV.iii.11) and the country's most powerful politician, has nevertheless served a stretch of indeterminate length in the Tower. He is angry and Richard assumes a curiously respectful, emollient tone as he encourages Hastings's bitterness towards the Queen's faction. Hastings's self-association with 'the eagle' in contrast to parvenu 'kites and buzzards' (ll. 132–3) reveals a man confident in his status, and his insider position within the establishment is confirmed by his knowledge of the King's condition – one would have thought that the unsequestered Richard would know more. Richard's entertaining mock piety and prim tut-tutting at the King's self-degradation draws no response from Hastings – is he wary of speaking of his master in this way, or might Hastings, who is after all sharing a woman (Mistress Shore) with the King, disapprove of Richard's moral sententiousness? There is a small gap in which the Hastings actor silently reacts, before Richard supplies the direct question 'What, is he in his bed?' (l. 142), to which Hastings gives the tersest of answers before exiting towards further liberty.

144 to the end   The stage is Richard's once again. Few actors will resist the slight beat before 'I hope' that guarantees laughter in the dark of the auditorium (l. 144). Things are going well. Barely minutes after he has revealed his master plan to set his brothers against each other, one is imprisoned and the other is bed-ridden. But, lest our sense of narrative expectation be too quickly sated, Richard introduces a new idea:

> For then I'll marry Warwick's youngest daughter –
> What though I killed her husband and her father?
>
> (ll. 152–3)

More laughter in the dark. Here Richard (like Iago after him) gestures towards then denies us exact knowledge of his motivation. Already habituated to the role of Richard's confidant, the audience is now teased with uncertainty. Why *does* Richard want to marry 'Warwick's youngest daughter'? Not for love, but 'for another secret close intent' (l. 157) – after so much brazen candour in his moments alone with us thus far, the coyness is strange and tantalizing. He wants us to want more.

Act I, scene ii

1–30   Shakespeare's plays are designed to flow and all scene divisions are, to a certain extent, artificial. The stage is probably never empty; like white noise during a radio transmission, an empty stage is *generally* anathema to directors and actors, and unnerving for an audience (it can of course be used intentionally to this effect). As Richard turns to leave, we should imagine, before he has left the stage, another body of movement to distract the eye: a woman in black, a hearse and attendants. We have heard three women mentioned so far – Mistress Shore, the Queen, and Warwick's daughter – but the costume of mourning and the presence of the corpse both suggest that the woman we now see before us has been on the losing side of the recent civil war. As with the guard that escorted Clarence to the Tower, Shakespeare has left the number of coffin bearers and guards open to interpretation and the human resources

of the theatre company. In *Hamlet*, Claudius regrets that he buried
Polonius 'in hugger mugger' (IV.v.82); might there be something
equally lacking in pomp in this pathetic procession? For the woman,
the ceremony is going too quickly, too cursorily: 'Set down, set down
your honourable load' (l. 1). The identities of corpse and mourner are
immediately established: Henry VI (whom Richard has stabbed in the
Tower – indicating that the procession, although 'coming' from St
Paul's (l. 28), might enter from that side of the stage into which
Clarence has vanished, to confirm the association between Richard's
victims) and 'poor **Anne**', the quarry first mentioned in the closing
lines of Richard's last monologue. Richard, who has been off stage for
seconds, is already the subject of fierce attention, as Anne offers the
first of the play's many curses (ll. 14ff.).

The challenge for the actor playing Anne is to shift the mood from
Richard's opening rationality and deceit towards an emotional
climate of sincere suffering. She must go speedily from 0 to 60, as it
were, from controlled mourning to angry, tearful lamentations over
the body. (By the end of the scene, she will be in reverse gear, but that
will only be fully appreciated if she begins with accelerative anger.)
This is a long speech, which may be delivered to her onstage audience
(what are *their* attitudes to laying down the hearse: reluctant? respectful? more than their job's worth?) or may be an intensely internalized
fantasy of revenge. She bids the bearers take up the hearse again –
'And still as [whenever] you are weary of the weight / Rest you,
whiles I lament King Henry's corpse' (ll. 29–30) – an instruction
which gracefully displaces her distress – the reason for the procession halting – onto the coffin bearers' weariness, while also perhaps
implying that there aren't enough of them to carry the hearse
comfortably.

31–65   Richard's entrance is abrupt and commanding. He seems to
announce his arrival with his voice from the margins of the stage. Is
it his royal status or his physical threat – or both – that cowers Anne's
male entourage? Does Richard strike to the ground and kick the
gentleman whose brave, lonely protest is the only resistance offered
to him (l. 36)? The hearse is laid down again and the corpse responds
in fine melodramatic fashion by bleeding afresh (ll. 53–4). Anne, who

has presumably removed the shroud to reveal this spectacle, invites her onstage audience to bear witness; their presence throughout the ensuing dialogue should be kept in the reader's mind: how conscious are the antagonists, Richard and Anne, of the onlookers?

66–142 Everything is now set for the main event. Richard's improbable – and apparently gratuitous – task is to seduce Anne in the vicinity of, if not over, her father-in-law's dead body. What follows is a highly patterned dialogue which, while stilted and implausible on the page, springs to life on stage when the actors use the repetitions and inversions ('divine perfection'/'diffused infection', 'Fairer than tongue'/'Fouler than heart', ll. 73, 76, 79, 81) as charged units of kinetic energy, proof that the two are listening intently to each other's choice of words and rhythms of speech. The interchange (at least between lines 66 and 112) is consistently up-tempo, two minds working quickly, sometimes finishing each other's sentences:

> I did not kill your husband.
>> Why then he is alive.
>
>   (l. 89)

Richard's excuses are specious, mischievous and shamelessly false: I didn't kill your husband and father-in-law . . . well, maybe I did . . . but they provoked me . . . and I did them a favour by sending them to Heaven. Is Richard intentionally fuelling her indignation or does he underrate his opponent? The first mention of sex ('Your bedchamber', l. 109) seems to wrong-foot Anne. Although clearly revolted, she gives her weakest contribution to the battle so far ('I hope so', l. 112) and Richard seizes on this uninspired moment by self-consciously altering the tempo of the scene. He wants the 'keen encounter' over and to 'fall somewhat into a slower method', a method that will better suit the pseudo-Petrarchan flattery he is about to lavish on her beauty. He now adds an unlikely new shade to his palette, that of the wooer, a role for which his body, so he has told us, makes him singularly miscast. Her response to his relatively *legato* compliments is to try to shift back to the *staccato* of the keen encounter. In this she is successful, but as their words increasingly tread on each other's heels,

their bodies are compelled together, until her only option is primi-
tive and unequivocal:

> Where is he?
>   Here.
>   *She spitteth at him*
>   Why dost thou spit at me?
>
>   (l. 142)

We should not be deceived by 'at'; she may well hit the target and her
saliva hang from his face.

143–78 Although Anne's responses remain defiant – 'Out of my
sight, thou dost infect my eyes' (l. 146) – the audience might begin to
wonder why she doesn't terminate the interview. Does she gesture at
some point to the coffin bearers to pick up the hearse, thus inviting
them to break into the magnetic field in which she and Richard
have been sparring? Or is there something compulsive and addictive
about this argument and this antagonist that makes it impossible to
leave?

When does Anne begin to buckle? The actor is faced with a noto-
riously difficult job in revealing the seismic shift in her character.
Later, Anne reflects on how, 'in so short a space, my woman's heart /
Grossly grew captive to his honey words' (IV.i.74–5). It seems that
Anne is saddled with this sexist explanation of her behaviour. The
question remains: which short space and which combination of
honey words seals the coup? Perhaps the spit on his face has
reminded Richard of tears, for now, as with Clarence, he makes a
display of weeping. 'Those eyes of thine from mine hath drawn salt
tears' (l. 151). 'Hath' is ambiguous: does Richard mean Anne's beauty
has for some time afflicted him with tears, or – more theatrically – is
he referring to newly sprung tears? If so, Richard sobs his pathetic
way through the ensuing lines – the Folio contains twelve further
lines, in which Richard protests his historical inability to cry – but, in
a rare stage direction describing facial expression, Anne is apparently
unmoved: '*She looks scornfully at him*' (after l. 156). The tears have not
worked. A new approach is needed. The 'sharp-pointed sword'
Richard now presents to Anne is an horrific object: was it not this

blade that penetrated her husband and father-in-law? It is now thrust into her hand and, in a deeply confusing and unexpected gambit, Richard reveals his naked chest and invites her to plunge the blade. For a second all is still as the audience registers this striking image, a kneeling man utterly at the mercy of an armed woman. What will she do? In a spasm, the sword moves towards but does not find flesh. Perhaps his voice – 'Nay, do not pause' – halts its trajectory, or perhaps she simply cannot kill the thing she is beginning, inexplicably, to love. The *Nay/But, Nay/But* see-saw of Richard's lines (ll. 165–9) seems to suggest a parallel sword movement, an alternation between two levels of tension that will be visible in both bodies. It is equally possible that the sword's point remains rigidly pressed against his skin until the tension can hold no longer and she drops the weapon. An outrageous, nonsensical injunction follows:

> Take up the sword again, or take up me.
>
> (l. 169)

Richard feels sufficiently confident instantly to bring the sword back into play by threatening suicide in front of her. ('Tush, that was in thy rage' can get a laugh, but this will dissipate tension; it is also a clue line: Anne's rage has by this point in the scene been replaced by a more bewildered, complex emotional state.) 'I would I knew thy heart' (l. 178) is the sound of Anne signing her own death warrant.

179–212 Replacing his sword – or at least putting it out of harm's way – Richard introduces a new, highly symbolic prop: 'Vouchsafe to wear this ring' (l. 187). Has he been wearing the ring? The rhythm of the clipped, almost entirely monosyllabic short lines between them (ll. 178–88) is that of a thrust and parry, but when Anne receives the ring the luxuriant, elongated cadence of Richard's lines – the open vowel of 'look', the polysyllabic 'encompasseth' – signals his victory. Does he have her hand in his? Does the tenderness of the touch, after so much violent interaction with the sword, somehow melt her into silence? If the ring exchange has been sensual, Richard assumes a dignified, penitential persona for the remainder of the interview. At the opening of the scene, a few minutes ago, she was inseparable

from the corpse – the procession was suspended in order for her obse-
quies. Now, apparently convinced by Richard's solemnity, she leaves
the body with its assassin. Her exit lines (ll. 208–10) are elliptical and
can be played as intentionally enigmatic, residually hostile or down-
right flirtatious. She is accompanied by two gentlemen. Richard and
some servants remain. The promise to inter the corpse at Chertsey
monastery is broken, and he sends the servants and body to
Whitefriars. (Whitefriars, although in historical fact a priory, might
for the purposes of comedy be delivered as if it were somewhere far
from sanctified: 'No, to Slough' might be a contemporary analogue.)

213 to the end   He is alone again. What does he want to share with
us with regard to the spectacle we have just witnessed? Amazement
and incredulity at having achieved the impossible? Or irrepressible
glee and self-satisfaction? It is still not clear why Richard has wooed
Anne; perhaps for no other reason than for Shakespeare to show us
his power as a performer. It is, as it were, art for art's sake. Richard
reviews this performance in one long, accumulative sentence (ll.
216–23) in which he relishes listing the obstacles he has just over-
come. A brief pause is allowed for this to sink in, and then the coda –
'Ha' (l. 223) – which might be delivered as an interrogative ('Well, isn't
that incredible?') or as an expression of triumph ('Yes!'). This line is
extrametrical – Richard's exuberance is bursting beyond the regularity of blank verse. The speech's second section (ll. 224–35) effectively
amplifies the first in detailing the virtues of Anne's dead husband and
the improbable amnesia that has let her succumb to the charm of his
murderer. The comically glib ('whom I some three months since /
Stabbed in my angry mood at Tewkesbury', ll. 225–6) gives way to the
heightened register of the encomium, as he takes a perverse pleasure
in praising his victim (ll. 227–30). In drawing attention to his own gait
and body (l. 235), Richard leaves the main theme of the speech – the
improbability of his success with Anne – to indulge in some cod
narcissism: 'I'll be at charges for a looking-glass' (l. 240). The first
scene of the play has ended with Richard's resolution to divide his
brothers and to marry Anne. Alone with us now, as he was then, he
has no thought for Edward and Clarence – nothing is allowed to
cloud the exuberance of his spirits. He is even looking forward to

reprising the recent role (l. 246). His closing couplet and exit are radiant with the thrill of the chase.

Act I, scene iii

1–41   After the series of monologues and focused exchanges from which Shakespeare creates his opening two scenes, we are now plunged into the more diffuse, chaotic and densely peopled world of the court. From the shady no-man's-lands in which Richard has lurked and operated, we move to the locus of power. Control of this space is vital. How do we know this is the court? From Rivers's opening lines, a model of succinct scene-setting, we can strongly infer that the woman he is addressing is the **Queen**. Although it is not registered in the dialogue, **Rivers** is the Queen's brother and **Grey** (also, confusingly, later referred to as **Dorset**) her son from her first marriage, and the performers may choose to signal this by physically comforting their sister and mother, an easy intimacy that would, of course, be unlikely between the Queen and non-relations. Her apparently distressed, impatient entrance marks a strong overlapping contrast with Richard's confident, complacent exit, and the provisional finality of Richard's closing couplet is broken by the Woodville family's mid-conversational momentum. We quickly learn that, given the King's perilous health, the state is on the verge of crisis. **Buckingham** and **Stanley Earl of Derby** – two key players in the ensuing action – enter and the latter is immediately wrong-footed by the Queen's accusation of his wife's treachery. This sets the tone of accusation, denial and counter-accusation in which this long scene is saturated. Buckingham, typically for this master politician, is neutral and emollient ('Madam, good hope', 'Madam, we did', ll. 34, 36). Buckingham's mention of the Duke of Gloucester (l. 37), as so often in this play, effectively heralds the entrance of that character.

41–102   Richard enters in mock high-dudgeon – he may also, depending on the actor's interpretation, have kept his promise to entertain a score or two of tailors (I.ii.241), and have changed into a more fashionable costume since his wooing of Anne. Although neither Q nor F provide an entry for Hastings, it is most plausible he enters here. Richard's rant might begin as the butt-end of a conversation with Hastings ('They do me wrong and I will not endure it', l. 42), then, finding himself in the midst of 'them', he neatly segues into a general attack on those present. Rivers's question (l. 54) is surely faux naive, an invitation to Richard to cut to the chase. In the first two scenes of the play, we have seen Richard the flatterer, the smiling deceiver, the cogger (all of which he professes himself incapable of here); now we see the brawler (see l. 324) attempting to drive a series of wedges between the King, his family by marriage, and the various noblemen–politicians – especially Stanley and Hastings – who might distrust the extent of the Queen's influence. The impression is one of bustle on Richard's part, the natural vigour of the lines seeming to demand a physical hyperactivity. The stage could be composed of at least two groupings – most likely the Queen's family on one side, the noblemen on the other – and Richard works these two audiences.

The Queen, in making the contrast between Richard's 'interior hatred' and 'outward actions' (ll. 65–6), reinforces the sense that, unlike Clarence, she has no illusions about Richard's real nature and intentions. This is a long-standing, tired argument (cf. l. 106) given new life by the King's illness and the ominous issue of succession. What is Richard's relationship with Buckingham at this point? Should the actors reveal the two men's sympathy straight away? Might Richard seek Buckingham's – or perhaps Hastings's – complicit approval of the class-conscious lines about jacks being made gentlemen (ll. 70–4)? If this is addressed to one of the noblemen, it nevertheless has the desired effect of provoking the Queen. 'God grant that we never may have need of you' (l. 76) has an air of finality about it, as if she wanted to draw a line under this current squabble. She might even attempt an exit here, an exit checked by Richard, who is hungry for further brawling. His cross-examination (ll. 90–1) prompts Rivers to step forward in the Queen's defence. The cumulative sarcasm of the 'she may/may she' repetitions and the pun on 'marry' show Richard's mind in full improvisational gear (ll. 93–102) as he seems to dumbfound Rivers.

103–57 It is up to the actor playing Elizabeth to decide whether the lines 'I had rather be a country servant maid / Than a great queen with this condition' (ll. 107–8) are sincere or, alternatively, a hollow self-indulgence, a lady-cum-Queen protesting too much at the pitfalls of the altitude to which fortune has raised her. Much will depend on the ways in which the Woodville family is portrayed in general. Is there evidence in their dress of their relishing their recent elevation? Are they conspicuous consumers? How much of the *arrivisme* that Richard satirizes is apparent in the way they bear themselves? Does Margaret's later description of Elizabeth as a 'painted queen' (l. 241) indicate narcissism or an excessive concern for preening?

At the end of the Queen's speech our attention is caught by a new figure. Her entrance has been unheralded and unnoticed by those who are at this point 'snarling' and 'Ready to catch each other by the throat' (ll. 185–6). 'Old' **Queen Margaret** will be a familiar figure to anyone seeing *Richard III* in the context of the *Henry VI* plays; outside that context, she is a mysterious, almost spectral presence here now. Although she makes her claim to the throne explicit in her first aside, there should be a sense of incongruity about this, in the same way that Gogol's diary-keeping Madman claims to be the King of Spain. She is distinct from those on stage both by age and in the presumed shabbiness of her appearance – she has been in exile, evidently without the material benefits enjoyed of royalty. Margaret's long series of asides pose a staging challenge. It has been suggested that the asides might be heard but ignored by the wrangling court, but this makes little sense; when Margaret wants to be heard, she makes sure of it (l. 158) and the revelation of her presence clearly affects the onlookers (l. 160). The difficulty is not so much with naturalism; audiences are happy to accept the convention of the aside, even at this length. More germane are questions of placing and pace. For the former, it is likely that Margaret either holds a static position or works round the periphery of the playing space. In terms of pace, there is a disjunction between the escalating momentum of the main action's dispute and the potentially deadening effect of Margaret's interjections. The latter can either be pruned or, if completely retained, should be quick and darting.

In a play so preoccupied with memory and the past, the spat between Richard, Rivers and the Queen entertainingly reopens old wounds. Richard is on the offensive. Margaret's asides punctuate a

twenty-four-line speech of his in which he further provokes the
Queen by reminding her 'What you have been ere now, and what you
are; / Withal, what I have been, and what I am' (ll. 132–3). Aggression
is combined with mock piety ('which Jesu pardon', l. 136) and sham
compassion ('I am too childish-foolish for this world', l. 142). In stat-
ing that he 'had rather be a pedlar' than king, is Richard satirizing the
Queen's 'country servant maid'? Elizabeth's restated claim that she is
deeply unhappy to be queen is the final straw for the women she
replaced, and Margaret reveals herself to the court by stepping out of
the margins.

158–260   The entrance is shocking, although it is hard to say
whether Margaret's use of 'trembles' actually describes the physical
response of the court or whether she is claiming that they *should* be
reacting to her presence with quakes and shivers. Richard, for one,
does not want to look at her (l. 163). The sight of her, as he quickly
reveals, has reminded him of his father's death at her hands and his
rebuke unites the court in indignation. If they have so far been
cowed by Margaret's arrival, they seem to find strength now,
inspired by a common scapegoat to forget current wrangling and
to turn all their hatred on the Lancastrian (ll. 179–84, 187). The
Yorkists are pulling together. The memory of 'York's dread curse' (l.
188) heralds the series of curses from Margaret that will return to
haunt each of their recipients. The absent King Edward, the Queen,
Rivers, Dorset and Hastings are all cursed in turn (ll. 194–211). What
can we infer from their silence in the face of these dire predictions?
How seriously do they take Margaret's maledictions? Might they
laugh them off as the ravings of a crazed old woman, or,
conversely, is their silence indicative of appalled fear? It is left to
Richard to interrupt (l. 212) and he appears to be on the point of
departure ('Stay, dog', l. 213): have her curses unnerved him? She
has stored up the lioness's share of her invective for him and she
gets so carried away with her apparently endless supply of epithets
('Thou . . . Thou . . . Thou') that she forgets the main purpose of her
speech. The quick-witted substitution of her name for his (l. 231)
takes the wind from her sails – the court might well be delighted
and relieved to have Margaret's authoritative domination of the

stage punctured so effectively. It certainly imbues Hastings, Rivers
and Dorset with the confidence finally to answer back to Margaret
– Hastings offers physical violence (l. 248), while Dorset, less hot-
headedly, simply writes her off as 'lunatic' (l. 254).

261–323   Richard allows the recent argument with the Queen's
family to reignite (l. 261). His majestic allusion to his high birth is
designed to provoke them further, but Margaret, developing the
imagery of light, shade and nesting, returns the focus to her own
losses. Her appeal to God (l. 271) might replicate an action (looking
up, kneeling, hands clasped in prayer) that previously initiated her
curses, and Buckingham, perhaps sensing another deluge, intervenes (l. 273). His garments alone are not spotted with Lancastrian
blood – if he accepts the offer, she even kisses his hand (l. 280).
There is a new tone here – for the first time Margaret speaks
warmly to another – she offers 'gentle counsel' (l. 297) and it might
be that she and Buckingham move forward, as if to speak confi-
dentially. Richard is described as *'yonder* dog' and his question,
'What doth she say, my lord of Buckingham?' (l. 295), makes most
sense if Margaret and Buckingham have spoken just out of earshot.
Whatever intimacy is achieved is smashed by Buckingham's icy
response (l. 296), a formal announcement of his loyalty to Richard.
She recoils from him, offers a prophecy that will stick deep in his
memory, and then departs with a general curse on the entire
company. The sense of relief following her exit is palpable.
Hastings and Rivers reveal that they, at least, have been genuinely
chilled by her curses (ll. 304–5). Richard is keen to return the
conversation to the topic of Clarence's imprisonment (l. 313). This
is the most divisive and inflammatory issue at court; his hope that
'God pardon them that are the cause of it' (l. 315) might be slyly
directed to Hastings, given that we have recently heard both men
blaming the Queen for these high-profile incarcerations (I.i.130–1).
Catesby enters. He will play an important part in Richard's rise to
power, but this future role is not hinted at in this brief entrance, the
function of which is to remind us of the offstage King and to clear
the stage. Given the King's condition, there is some urgency to his
call, and the court leaves hurriedly.

324 to the end   Richard stays: he has two appointments. The first
is with us. As at the close of the previous scene, he has the urge to
review his performance. Interestingly, his account of the preceding
events omits (or represses) Margaret. For him, she is a fragment of the
past, and his mind dwells only on the future and the passage to the
crown. On a basic level, the speech celebrates the brazen hypocrisy
of his dealings with the court. But it also reveals Richard's complete
contempt for those around him – even Buckingham is seen as one of
the 'simple gulls' (l. 328). Richard enjoys the saintly persona so much
that he even briefly revives the role for us; 'God bids us do good for
evil' (l. 335) might be delivered in the priestly voice with which
Richard has uttered previous 'odd ends stol'n out of holy writ' (l. 337).
The entrance of two men reminds Richard of his second appoint-
ment. The costumes of these men will certainly set them apart from
the Dukes and Earls who have just quit the stage, although that is not
to insist that they must be, say, working-class, or that they both come
from the same social sphere. Furthermore, their manner of entering
the playing area might indicate their unfamiliarity with these new
surroundings. Before we need conjecture any further, Richard
announces their identities to us: 'soft, here come my **executioners**'
(l. 339). Neither Q nor F distinguishes between the two men, and it is
up to the director to decide how to distribute the two speeches (ll.
342–3, 350–2). They are business-like; there is nothing to prepare us
for the comedic vein they will introduce to the following scene.
Richard is convinced of their professionalism – 'I like you, lads.
About your business' (l. 354) – and the scene concludes with the
Executioners and Richard exiting, presumably in separate directions:
they perhaps to that side of the stage associated with the Tower and
Clarence, and Richard towards the exit through which the court has
left to attend the King.

Act I, scene iv

1–76   The assassins' 'business' enters as they leave. Clarence, a good
deal more haggard and prison-stained since we met him in the opening scene, enters with either (a) an anonymous 'Keeper' (in F) or (b)
Brackenbury, the civil servant we have previously seen escort him to

the Tower (in Q). In F, Brackenbury will enter after line 68, speak lines 69–76, then exit with the Keeper on the arrival of the Executioners. Q, in conflating the characters, heightens the scene's intimacy, but also makes 'Sorrow breaks seasons and reposing hours . . .' (ll. 69ff.), spoken over the sleeping Clarence, a choric statement directly derived from the experience of having heard Clarence's nightmare. The director must decide.

If Clarence is not to sleep on the floor, a stage property such as a bench, couch, or at least a chair, must be brought on between scenes. (In Q, Brackenbury describes Clarence as *sitting* asleep (l. 87), in F he is *lying* asleep.) The general challenge in this scene is to create a claustrophobic, dank atmosphere, and the institutional quality of the props and Clarence's costume – combined with focused lighting – will do much to achieve this. The scene, as Wolfgang Clemen points out, is 'a tragedy in miniature with a dramatic curve complete in itself' (p. 64) and is divided into two, strongly contrasted movements, the second of which is marked by the arrival of the Executioners. Clarence's relation of his dream – after the high-pitched bickering of the court – ushers in an unprecedented note of melancholy reflection, a slackening of tempo in which the drama is internalized rather than interpersonal. In Act I, scene iii, the audience's eyes have flitted around the stage from speaker to speaker and from one appalled recipient of Margaret's curses to another. Here, our gaze narrows and focuses on one man. Clarence's great speech – one is tempted to write 'aria' – is dramaturgically straightforward but a test for the actor, who must convey the agony and suffering of a remorse-stricken conscience.

The effect of Clarence's narrative is complicated, if not contradictory. On the one hand, we, knowing he probably has only a short time to live, sympathize with the hallucinogenic unhappiness of his final moments, whilst also finding his richly sensitive personality attractive when compared with the worldlier, materialist concerns of the characters that have so far peopled the stage. On the other hand, the imagined encounters with his father-in-law, Warwick, and Prince Edward remind us of the 'false, fleeting, perjured Clarence' (l. 52) of the *Henry VI* plays, a far less attractive, morally compromised figure. The dream narrative has an interesting coda:

O Brackenbury, I have done these things
Which now bear evidence against my soul
For Edward's sake, and see how he requites me.

(ll. 63–5)

The actor might be horrified to admit '*I have done these things*', but the suspended sense of the sentence implies that it is anger at his ungrateful brother ('and see how he requites me') rather than his own guilt *per se* that wearies, even irritates Clarence. In F, following line 66, he prays to God that if He will be revenged on Clarence's 'misdeeds', Clarence's wife and children will be spared. Q, omitting this moment of concern, leaves open the possibility of a more self-centred character, one who goes to sleep cursing his brother's baffling behaviour rather than fearing God's justice. Brackenbury, however, is sympathetic enough towards Clarence's plight to offer to us a small choric poem on the conventional theme – beloved of Shakespeare – of the sufferings of those in power (ll. 69–76). In F, the reverie is broken by the First Executioner's (possibly offstage) shout, 'Ho, who's here?' In Q, the Executioners enter silently, perhaps at the end of Brackenbury's speech, leaving him to turn and be surprised by their presence. He certainly sounds shocked to have company and their appearance is clearly not reassuring.

77–189   It is hard to avoid the fact that the two Executioners are intended to be funny. This is one of those incursions of low comedy into the sacred space of tragedy that made parts of Shakespeare so distasteful to neo-classical critics. Shakespeare, whose theatrical instincts were significantly more sophisticated than those of his detractors, knew that by this point the scene needed oxygen, a 'breathing-while' (I.iii.60) for the Stygian gloom of the nightmare to dissipate, only to allow the tension eventually to build once again with renewed energy. At the close of Act I, scene iii, the two men have, as it were, their act together: taciturn professionals, they impress their patron with their dour determination. At Brackenbury's exit, however, The Professionals morph into Laurel and Hardy. While the ensuing dialogue treats some of the play's abiding serious themes – namely, conscience and damnation – the tone is light, unhurried, interludic. So unhurried, in fact, that the Second Executioner may well actually count to twenty after line 108 in the dogged attempt to rid himself of the last dregs of conscience. His disquisition on the word (like those of Falstaff on 'honour' and Iago on 'reputation' in later Shakespeare plays) is a comic deconstruction and one which prompts the brief twist of the hitherto resolute First Executioner having a twinge of guilt (ll. 133–4). At last united in the resolve to knock Clarence further unconscious, then drown him 'in the malmsey butt in the next room' (ll. 142–3), they are surprised when their victim wakes up.

If a performance of this scene is to be fully effective, the horse-play must now be set aside, as the two worlds – that of Clarence and of the Executioners – merge to create a life-and-death scenario. The comic hesitations of the Second Executioner have been replaced by a severity of tone that causes Clarence to comment on the thunderous, dark and deadly quality of his voice (ll. 151, 153). But for the scene to have any tension there must be a shadow of doubt in both murderers' minds over the justice of their commission: when neither can pronounce the word 'murder' (l. 155) we know that the death of Clarence is not a *fait accompli*. As if he sleepily half-overheard their previous talk of judgement days and damnation, Clarence immediately appeals to theological edict and to the sixth commandment (l. 178). But Laurel and Hardy know their history and they are firmly united in their disgust with Clarence's treachery during the War of the Roses. Their unity, the rising sense of them ganging-up, is expressed by their enthusiasm to continue and finish each other's sentences:

> And with thy treacherous blade
> Unrip'st the bowels of thy sovereign's son –
> Whom thou wert sworn to cherish and defend.

> (ll. 187–9)

190 to the end   Clarence's argument that revenge should be left to God is deftly and perceptively rebutted by the First Executioner, who points out that in stabbing Prince Edward at Tewkesbury, Clarence didn't hang around for God's judgement. There is perhaps here a growing sense of irritation on the part of the Executioners with the sophistry and hypocrisy of Clarence's pleas, an irritation that somehow whets their appetite for the job in hand. They might be pushing and shoving him about the stage, enjoying their physical domination over him, the cornered quarry. Are they both amused by Clarence's unwittingly ironic claim that Richard will reward them for sparing his life? Their simultaneous answers suggest so (ll. 214, 220). In F, the Second Executioner has the line 'Make peace with God, for you must die, my lord' (l. 229), which makes more dramatic sense than Q's attribution. By appealing explicitly to the 'holy feeling' in the Second's soul, Clarence appears to hit the raw nerve that leads to his indecision: 'What shall we do?' (l. 236). Clarence, as Richard predicted, is speaking well and makes the bold move of exclusively entreating one assassin whilst turning his back on the other. Once again, Q and F present alternatives. In Q, Clarence's final entreaty is cut short by the First Executioner's dagger; in F, the tension builds further with five more lines of pleading, followed by the Second's cry 'Look behind you, my Lord', allowing the grim possibility that Clarence turns round only to receive a stab in the stomach. Although in Q, the stage direction '*He stabs him*' appears between lines, as it were, the dagger thrusts are clearly meant to be timed with 'thus, and thus'. With the exception of Richard's defeat in battle at the end of the play, this is the only onstage death in *Richard III*. Its brutality must stand in for all those offstage demises engineered by Richard in subsequent Acts. It is 'desperately performed' (l. 245) and it is up to the fight choreographer to decide whether this means that Clarence struggles, and indeed whether he is still alive when he is dragged or carried off to be drowned 'in the next room' (l. 244). The Second Executioner is left alone to express his remorse. Is his speech underscored by Clarence's offstage yells and death throes? The First, quickly re-entering, upbraids his colleague for his cowardice. He is presumably splashed with malmsey, giving him a gory, blood-stained appearance. The Second exits hastily, leaving the First to conclude the scene with a blunt couplet and his exit towards Clarence's still warm corpse.

ACT II

Act II, scene i

Entry   A brass fanfare blows across the crime scene and the stage is transformed from prison to court. Our first sight of **King Edward**, 'sick', possibly leaning on his wife for support, is not of the wanton playboy. What does Edward's appearance reveal about his reign and court? Might we feel some sympathy with Richard's desire to be king if the present incumbent is desiccated by lust and/or decrepit? The surrounding protagonists are familiar faces by now; '*and others*', once again, gives permission to the director to swell the scene with an indeterminate number of attendant lords, probably the same actors who carried and guarded the hearse in Act I, scene ii, who have had more than ample time for costume changes. In the interests of time and fluidity, there is no need for Clarence's chair or bench to be struck (i.e. removed from the stage). With a rich drape it can be covered and transformed into a throne, or even more simply, with no change at all, can 'become' with the audience's imaginative consent, Edward's sickbed. As Jowett points out, 'this would visually reinforce the brothers' shared proximity to death' (p. 209n).

1–44   The mood – if only superficially – is bright and amicable. Although Edward speaks of having '*done* a good day's work' (l. 1), perhaps the most important work – the reconciliation of the court's rival factions – remains to be accomplished. Once the King is settled comfortably he instigates a ritual of handshaking, hand-kissing and embraces involving Hastings and the Queen's faction. It seems likely that, on entering, the court has divided spatially along party lines. The first encounter between Rivers and Hastings is clearly forced, uncomfortable and phoney, as Edward angrily reprimands the pair for dallying before their sovereign (ll. 11–15). In the remaining reconciliations, there is a strong sense of speech through clenched teeth, of barely suppressed hatred. The antagonists know they are simply humouring the King and that in his absence (or at his death) normal service will resume. Is it a sign of the weakening of Edward's mental faculties – brought on by whatever disease is killing him – that he fails to perceive anything wrong in the remaining reconciliations? That Buckingham is asked to join the love-in is perhaps a surprise for the audience. Nothing he has said or done so far has revealed tendentiousness. The extravagance of his speech is a clear, if not heavy-handed, indication of his 'deep, hollow, treacherous' nature, and his self-curse is clearly meant to echo Anne's (I.ii.24–6).

45–93   In *Richard III*, when a character's absence is noted, you can be quite sure he'll enter within seconds, or 'in good time' (l. 45). After almost exactly the same interval before he burst into the first court scene – forty or so lines – Richard again arrives, injecting pace into a scene that has just found its equilibrium. In contrast to his earlier peevishness, here he is jocund, the picture of bonhomie. Clarence is dead and Richard has reason to be cheerful. Without prompting, he works his way round the 'princely heap' (a beautifully judged oxymoron), commanding the stage space with energetic mock piety. His closing 'I thank my God for my humility' (l. 71) is such an outrageous sham it can only be meant for us, his audience, or possibly as a knowing aside to Buckingham. Once again, the scene achieves a moment of resolution and superficial harmony as the Queen speaks, apparently genuinely, of compounded strife. But, in a marked exception to the Absent Character Rule, when she mentions Clarence, we know the noble Duke is not about to bound on stage. Richard seizes his opportunity to reproach the Queen for her insensitivity and to announce the news of Clarence's death (ll. 76–9). They all '*start*', meaning a sudden involuntary movement of surprise, and each of the major characters (save Hastings) is given a line or two in which to express their shock. Edward reveals that he had indeed ordered Clarence's death – an important new piece of information that will explain his lacerating guilt – but that the order had been reversed. Richard cracks a joke with us about his disability then takes a side-swipe at the Queen's family (ll. 86–94).

94 to the end   Stanley, a notable absence in the scene so far, enters with urgency to beg a reprieve for a servant, an extraneous moment which serves no other purpose than to prompt the King's impassioned set piece. The dramatic function of this speech is to confirm in the audience's mind the link between Clarence's death and that of Edward, underscoring Richard's responsibility for both. This is the last burst of energy of a dying man, and a study in disintegration. What had seemed an underwritten and ineffectual role now truly reigns on stage. The angry interrogatives that punctuate the first third of the speech suggest a trajectory around the playing space as the unanswerable questions are posed to a succession of shamed and embarrassed listeners.

In a flash of awful clarity, Edward turns heavenwards before seeking the arm of Hastings, his best friend, to help him off stage. Once again, the stage direction allows latitude: '*Exeunt some with King and Queen.*' In F, Buckingham is definitely one of those left behind, as he has a line; others remain, too, as Richard addresses himself to 'Lords'. But in Q, there is the possibility of either (a) Richard and Buckingham alone for the first time, with Richard as it were sounding out Buckingham's political inclinations; or (b) Richard and any combination of named and/or anonymous Lords. In the case of (a), the closing line could be darkly ironic, an invitation to 'comfort' a man whom both want dead.

Act II, scene ii

1–87 The first sequence, though usually cut in performance, creates an important shift of emphasis. For the first time, we are presented with something like a domestic scene. The fourth line establishes that the old woman and two children we see before us are the **Duchess of York** (mother to Edward, Clarence and Richard), and Clarence's **Boy** and **Girl**. Again, the scene seems to begin with the continuation of an offstage conversation. Perhaps foreshadowing the imminent arrival of the Queen, the Duchess has entered in a state of distress; the attempt to hide the hand-wringing and breast-beating from the children has motivated the movement onto the stage. The children follow, curious and confused, in her wake. Although this scene as a whole will emphasize the grief and suffering caused directly or otherwise by Richard, it is not a maudlin spectacle. These are tough, battle-hardened people. In the Boy's call for God to revenge (l. 14) his father's death, we hear not only an echo of Richard's line in the previous scene (II.i.137), but also a chilling commitment to the cycle of violence and the ethos of retribution that has scarred the country throughout the first tetralogy.

Richard's propaganda is clearly working: the Boy blames Edward for Clarence's death, and his portrait of Richard hugging and weeping (ll. 22–3) amplifies our sense of Richard's touchy-feely avuncular persona, preparing us for his interaction with the Princes in Act III, scene i. As the Duchess seeks to disillusion the Boy, the conversation is interrupted by an offstage noise. In F, the Queen now enters, as in Act I, scene ii, with Rivers and Dorset; in Q, she is alone in raw grief. Q's emphasis is on women and children, F's on a broader concept of family. The Queen's hair, in keeping with early modern conventions for symbolizing extreme distress, is '*about her ears*'. Rather than the Duchess and the children rushing to comfort their daughter-in-law and aunt, their reactions are formidable, even frosty. In the first of the informal competitions in suffering that women play throughout *Richard III*, the Duchess observes that her grief is twice that of Elizabeth's. The children, too, emotionally and probably physically, keep their distance, refusing to mourn with her given her imputed role in the death of their father. There follows one of those highly patterned choric lamentations (cf. *Romeo and Juliet*, IV.iv) with which the modern naturalistic theatre is so uncomfortable. The series of questions (ll. 73–5) might be conceived of as addressed directly to other characters in an extension of the 'lowlier than thou' game. Alternatively, all these speeches might be more abstractly addressed, so that the audience is presented with the sight of three separate units of grief, each lost in its own misery. The Duchess breaks the keening with her 'Alas, I am the mother of these moans' (l. 79) – in the face of such suffering, her grandmaternal instincts seem to kick in and her invitation to Elizabeth and the children to pour all their tears on her, strongly implies that the units congeal to form one group of mourning. It is this sight – four of his victims' loved ones united in tears – which greets Richard as he enters. (Has he not seen his mother (see l. 92) because she has been obscured in this group embrace?)

88 to the end   As with the close of the previous scene, it is up to the director to decide who, apart from Buckingham, should join

Richard in this entrance. F has Stanley, Hastings and Ratcliffe, but Q
is unspecific. Buckingham later addresses 'You cloudy princes and
heart-sorrowing peers' (l. 99), so it probably makes sense to bring on
as much of the court as possible. The Duchess has already made clear
her disgust with her youngest son, and her pointed blessing (ll. 94–5)
prompts his aside, which, despite its obvious humour, might also
present an opportunity for a more psychologically-inclined Richard
to register pain and rejection. Perhaps sensing that the exchange has
thrown Richard from the political matter in hand, Buckingham steps
forward to entreat solidarity and to raise the practical issue of succession. Q, in cutting 18 lines here for the sake of pace, sacrifices the
tense passage in which Rivers queries the recommendation of 'some
little train' (l. 107) accompanying the Prince from Ludlow to London.
In Q, the smoothness with which Buckingham's suggestion is
accepted implies that he is perceived as a neutral councillor and
above suspicion; F creates the dramatically more interesting impression that his enmity towards the Queen's family is beginning to be
suspected. Glitch or no glitch, the court concludes the scene on a
note of unity, committed to fetching the Prince to London to be
crowned king. Maybe there is some scope in this exit, or during
Buckingham's speech, for some interaction between Richard and
Clarence's children, an image of consolation that might stick in the
audience's memory when Richard will, later in Act IV, dispose of
their claims to the crown. All leave, except for Buckingham and
Richard. Perhaps Richard is on his way off, when his new ally calls
him back with 'My lord' (l. 115). The reference to 'the story we late
talked of' (l. 118) confirms that the two have already forged a partnership while waiting in the wings, as it were, during the main stage
action. The effusive warmth of Richard's response adds a new hue to
the chameleon's skin: we have not yet heard Richard express genuine
admiration and gratitude. He is no longer alone.

Act II, scene iii

1 to the end   'What is the city but the people?' asks Sicinius in
Coriolanus (III.i.198). The national power-brokers and aristocratic elite
have – with the exception of the two Executioners – dominated

Richard III so far. Now, as their two most unscrupulous representatives leave the stage, their place is taken by what we might call 'real' people, remarkable in this play for their ordinariness. How the **Three Citizens** are characterized will largely depend on the production's overall locale and period. Are they all of one class or drawn from diverse walks of life, even different parts of the country, so that their meeting creates the image of a national microcosm? Where are they going? 'We are sent for to the Justice' says the Second Citizen (l. 46), but, as Jowett points out, it is not made clear exactly why: 'It might hint at the arming or mustering of a militia, or merely associate the Citizens with the administration of justice' (p. 227n). Like any truly baffling line in Shakespeare, this one can, of course, be rewritten. The most logical rewrite would be 'sent for to the Mayor' to anticipate the three Citizens' presence in the later scene (see Hankey, p. 153).

Generally speaking, short scenes increase the audience's feeling of the play's momentum. This – easily the shortest scene so far – is designed to convey both the headlong rush of events following Edward's death and the nationwide climate of fear and uncertainty when the throne is empty. Although the Second Citizen does his best to put a positive gloss on the situation, his views are outweighed by the bleaker pronouncements of the Third. His verdict that 'full of danger is the Duke of Gloucester' (l. 27) is interesting; if an anonymous citizen distrusts Richard, it is clear that his ascent to the throne might meet popular resistance. Yet, above all, the Third Citizen's catalogue of ominous proverbs help intensify the atmosphere of this phase of the play, a time of pivotal change for the plot – Edward and Clarence are dead – as much as for England. In a resonant allusion to the play's opening lines, we are darkly informed that 'winter is at hand' (l. 33).

Act II, scene iv

1–37 As elsewhere, the very first lines allow the audience a few seconds to become accustomed to the new scene before the key piece of information (in this case the chief referent of the opening line's 'they') is offered. The speaker, although never named, is clearly marked by his costume as a high ranking **member of the clergy**. But of the newcomers, the audience's eye is drawn to the child, **Young York**. His precocious banter will dominate the first half of the scene. (When the Queen calls her eldest child 'my son of York', we are again reminded of the play's opening.) In a play in which all characters are cursed with almost perfect memories, the discussion of the Princes' relative heights leads young York to remember Richard's mealtime proverbs (ll. 12–13). (Again, the register of the previous scene spills into this one; Richard's remembered adage also prepares us for his acid proverbial asides in Act III, scene i.) Young York's perkiness is juxtaposed with the tension of his mother. She is silent through much of the opening movement of the scene, apparently aloof and distracted from her son's dialogue with his grandmother. Although the elder Prince is not expected till 'tomorrow or next day' (l. 3), this is nevertheless a scene of limbo and of waiting. Talk of Richard, the children's official Protector, cannot help but make the Queen anxious. In recycling rumours of Richard's monstrous, mordant birth (ll. 27–8), Young York gives us a strong impression of the everyday malice aimed at Richard's body; to learn of Richard's freakishness is clearly part of the court's unofficial curriculum. Who *has* told him this story? Richard's 'nurse' (l. 32) is a transparent lie. Is he covering for the Queen, who has fed him on her knee with these stories? Either way, she has had enough of his prattle. Q has 'A perilous boy', an understandable alternative (not adopted by Jowett) given that these are dangerous words. Like the Scrivener's speech (III.vi), 'Pitchers have ears' (l. 37) is one of those moments in *Richard III* that evocatively suggest a police state, an airless world of surveillance and spies. She is the Queen of England, the head of state, and yet she fears being overheard.

38 to the end   The Queen's interruption is tantalizing. Before she has a chance to explain what she might mean in more depth, Dorset enters. (F has an unnamed Messenger deliver this news, breaking the largely domestic nature of the scene.) His announcement that he has bad news instantly prompts concern for the elder Prince. He has been on her mind since the opening of the scene: if he is in health, how can the news be bad? When we learn that it is 'The mighty dukes, Gloucester and Buckingham' who have committed Rivers, Grey and

Vaughan to prison we know that the incipient partnership that took
shape at the close of Act II, scene ii, has now congealed into a double
act. The arrest of the Queen's brother and son and of Vaughan
(whose name we have not heard before this, but who is presumably
a close ally of the Woodvilles) leads both Queen and Duchess to shift
the register of the scene to one of formal lamentation. Both apparently surrender to misery, the Queen looking forward with awful
clairvoyance to a bloody future (ll. 52–7), the Duchess reflecting on a
no less turbulent past (ll. 58–68). The decision is made to seek sanctuary. Is Elizabeth moved by the Duchess's offer to accompany them
(ll. 70–1)? The Cardinal ushers them off stage and towards safety.

ACT III

Act III, scene i

Entry   The last time we heard '*trumpets sound*' it was to herald the
arrival of the terminally ill King Edward. It is therefore appropriate
that they should now aurally prepare the way for his destined successor, Prince Edward. Given that Buckingham and Richard have previously spoken of journeying to the Prince (II.ii.115) and have succeeded
in despatching his entourage to Pomfret, it makes sense that the
mighty dukes accompany the future monarch on stage. If so, who
forms their reception committee? Q and F name only the Cardinal
and the vague '*others*', but the Cardinal has only just left the stage; his
immediate reappearance would be awkward, and as far as
Elizabethan dramaturgy is concerned, would be one of few exceptions that prove the rule that characters never re-enter directly after
an exit. Editors have long included Stanley in this entrance, conjec-
turing that an exit apparently for Dorset ('*Dor.*') at line 149 in Q is
more likely to be meant for Stanley, whose name might have been
abbreviated to '*Der.*' (for Derby). Given that Stanley has no lines in the
scene, the director can decide on the necessity of his presence.
Catesby does speak later in the scene, so this is our first prolonged
sight of someone who will prove to be one of Richard's most efficient
henchmen.

The permissiveness of '*others*' is, once again, an open invitation to interpretation. Is the Princes' arrival in London greeted with pomp and circumstance or with a thin smattering of nobles and bureaucrats? Richard and Buckingham's tactic so far has been to separate the Prince from benign influence. It would be entirely in keeping with this practice if they had only, as it were, tipped off a few anonymous politicians and a token Cardinal. Alternatively, they might want to sustain the illusion of business as usual and of due process and thus have organized the customary, elaborate trimmings befitting this state occasion.

1–35 Either way, the assembled company is not sufficient for the Prince, who complains of the paucity of uncles (l. 6). Is this an intentionally pointed remark? Does the Prince on some level suspect the abduction and imminent demise of his uncle Rivers? Does he suspect Richard of being behind his uncle Clarence's death, a death which provoked his father's terminal seizure? His response to Richard – 'God keep me from false friends, but they were none' (l. 16) – reveals an astute mind. In the Citizens' scene (II.iii), the Third Citizen had worried for 'that land that's governed by a child' (l. 11). The manner in which the Prince carries himself in this scene might indicate that England could (and will) do a lot worse than to have this child govern the land. The **Lord Mayor** of London's slightly tardy arrival increases the impression that this is a hastily improvised rather than a stage-managed occasion. Should he not have been waiting, on the spot, to welcome the future King to his capital? The Lord Mayor will play an important part in the middle section of the play and, although he has no further lines in this scene, the actor will want to establish a persona on his first entrance.

The Lord Mayor's arrival reminds the Prince of the absence of his mother and brother. Hastings enters, on cue, to inform them all of the Queen's decision to take sanctuary. The combined description of Hastings as 'slug' and 'sweating' (ll. 22, 24) here can be taken to signal a man past his physical prime; when we further remember his affair with Mistress Shore, the actor is faced with the clear potential to play him as a tubby sybarite. Yet, thin men can sweat, and who is to say that Hastings is not devotedly in love with Mistress Shore? If nothing else, the mention of 'sweating' here materializes the Prince's Hastings/haste pun (l. 22), as well as intensifying our sense of the unscripted nature of this ceremony. Interestingly, it is not Richard but Buckingham who responds first to Hastings's news. Is there a moment of confusion after line 30, in which Richard is clearly dumbfounded but, not wanting to break his present impersonation of the kind uncle, nods to Buckingham to take control of the situation? Buckingham's response is imperious and authoritative. In administering orders to both the Cardinal and Hastings, he is publicly flexing his political muscle.

36–94 The heavy-handed injunction that the young Prince should be plucked from his mother's arms (l. 36) puts both the Cardinal and Hastings in awkward positions; the former needs persuading of the ethical probity of breaking 'the holy privilege / Of blessed sanctuary' (ll. 40–1), while Hastings (as at I.i.142) has only the briefest of lines (l. 59) through which to communicate his attitude. Buckingham's argument – that the Prince is too young to know what sanctuary is and therefore cannot claim or deserve it – neatly sidesteps the question of why the Queen might have sought sanctuary in the first place.

After the departure of the Cardinal and Hastings, our attention narrows to the triangular dynamics between Buckingham, Richard and the Prince. It is still unclear exactly what the mighty dukes want to do with or to the child. Perhaps they are at a slight loss for conversation starters when left alone and it is the Prince – his impeccably-bred manners kicking in – who breaks the silence. The ensuing quizzing of Buckingham on the history of the Tower of London serves to foreground the themes of memory and posterity, to further reveal the Prince's precociousness, and to provide Richard (apparently standing apart from this conversation) with the opportunity for his sardonic asides, which, for the first time, explicitly announce his intention to murder his nephews.

95–149 When Hastings and the Cardinal re-enter with Young York, is there any evidence that he has been forcibly man-handled away from his mother, as Buckingham advised, should she resist? After the sombre exchange with his brother, his spirits do not appear

to be too dashed as he instantly reverts to the perilous/parlous badi-
nage of Act II, scene iv. In the annals of *Richard III*'s criticism, it is not
easy to find too many kind words about Young York. Hammond
speaks for many when he describes him as 'a most thoroughly dislike-
able brat' (p. 111). His long-suffering brother appears to agree (ll. 126–7).
(Of course, such a distinction between a wayward, irritating young
prince and his dignified elder brother seems remote to us now.) The
request to handle Richard's dagger – gratuitous in itself – prompts the
accelerative, punning exchanges that seem to culminate with 'How? /
Little' (ll. 124–5). Yet Young York cannot leave the cross-talk alone.
Despite the lack of stage direction here, the dramatic potential of
embodying the image of the apish boy on the hunchback's shoulders
is irresistible and has traditionally provided the Richard actor with an
exciting 'point', a climactic moment of character revelation which in
the pre-twentieth-century theatre would often be met with immediate
applause. If Young York does indeed leap on his uncle's back (at l. 131),
Richard has the option for the first time of showing us the lacerating
pain of his condition as the boy's weight applies an electric shock to
his torso. If such pain shades into rage, how quickly does Richard
suppress the understandable desire to 'give' the boy his dagger in the
most sinister sense of that verb? How does he cover his loss of self-
control? Perhaps it is Buckingham, characteristically, who comes to
the rescue with four lines of loaded praise (ll. 132–5). Jowett has these
as an aside to Hastings, but there is no reason why they should not be
addressed more generally. In 'So cunning and so young is wonderful'
we hear a strong echo of Richard's earlier 'So wise so young, they say,
do never live long' (l. 79), but now the line has been cleansed of sinister intent and sanitized for public consumption. If he ever lost it,
Richard regains his composure during these lines. As the Princes head
to the Tower (presumably exiting on that side of the stage into which
Clarence vanished in Act I, scene i), Prince Edward is once more given
an opportunity to show his acuity (ll. 146–7). Whatever our feelings
about his younger brother, there is potential to characterize the elder
Prince as a perspicacious, astute leader-in-waiting.

150 to the end After the subtextual tensions and double-speak of
the last few minutes, it is almost a relief to see the stage cleared for

some straightforward plotting. We need information. We know, of course, that Richard wants the crown, that Buckingham is now his chief spin-doctor, and that the Princes are under close supervision in the Tower. But what next? Richard seems happy to dwell on the memory of the 'little prating York' – his attribution of the Prince's 'bold, quick, ingenious, forward, capable' (l. 154) qualities to his mother might be a useful note for the actor playing Elizabeth. With a barely submerged hint at infanticide – 'Well, let them rest' (l. 156) – Buckingham steers him back on course, calling Catesby to join them downstage. Catesby's social standing is unclear, but as we will see, he moves comfortably among the most important aristocrats of the land and appears to be trusted by them all. Hastings will later call him 'my servant Catesby' (III.ii.20), although the sense probably means 'my representative' or 'one of my faction' – F, revealingly, has 'good friend' rather than 'servant'. Buckingham refers to Catesby as 'gentle', which might either recognize his breeding or be an ennobling epithet: he acts like a gentleman even if not born one. Either way, he will play an important part in the behind-the-scenes manoeuvring that will lift Richard to the throne.

It becomes clear that Hastings is perceived as the major obstacle to Richard's progress to the throne – on the purposed fate of the Princes, Richard and Buckingham are tantalizingly silent. Buckingham, again, takes charge, administering explicit instructions, to which Richard adds what is almost an afterthought (ll. 178–82). Richard's request to hear from Catesby 'ere we sleep' (l. 185) intensifies the audience's sense of escalating momentum: time is constricting and Richard's heart is beating faster. The mighty dukes are left alone in an echo of the close of Act II, scene ii. What happens, Buckingham asks, if Hastings is not tractable?

> Chop off his head, man. Somewhat we will do.
>
> (l. 190)

Options abound. Is Richard's spontaneous response jocular, psychopathic, or/and matter-of-fact? Is he surprised that Buckingham even needs to ask the question? That very strong mid-line caesura (or pause) might imply that he has gone too far. Has Buckingham responded with barely concealed surprise at the simple brutality of Richard's solution? Is it a premonition of the later moment when he will 'grow circumspect' (cf. IV.ii.31)? Or does he join in the joke, allowing their mutual enjoyment to fill the short space before 'Somewhat we will do'? If Richard does sense that Buckingham is squeamish at the prospect of assassination, might the ensuing offer of the earldom of Hereford be a direct encouragement to lay aside his qualms, just as, when the Second Executioner is troubled by 'conscience', the First Executioner reminds him of 'the Duke of Gloucester's reward' and greed triumphs over ethics? As we have seen, Richard increasingly appears to need Buckingham as his front man: such a need carries dangers for both men. Stabilizing this need by steering the conversation down the familiar track of financial reward, Richard manages to close the scene on a note of buoyant solidarity.

Act III, scene ii

1–32 As the Dukes exit complacently towards supper, an anonymous Messenger enters at speed. Whether he knocks on an actual door or any part of the stage wall, the sound of Hastings's voice from '*within*' (i.e. off stage) will signify that this scene takes place outside Hastings's house. We are primed for Catesby's visitation, but Stanley's messenger has got to Hastings first. He now enters and his appearance (hastily pulling on dressing gown? hair ruffled?) reveals a man dragged from a still-warm bed. It's four a.m. (For Jan Kott, this detail typifies Shakespeare's genius for suddenly projecting tragedy onto an everyday, domestic level: 'Who has not been awakened in this way at 4 a.m., at least once in his life?' p. 19.) We have heard that Hastings's opinion matters enormously to Stanley, that he will 'do all in all as Hastings doth' (III.i.167), but here we see Stanley attempting to reverse the direction of influence. The Messenger, faced with a man as unimaginative and bullish as Hastings, may be slightly embarrassed by his master's alarmist message, based as it is on the contents of a nightmare. 'The boar' is code for Richard – in this world where pitchers, even at four in the morning, have ears, he cannot refer to Gloucester by name. Hastings is offered the chance to save his own life – if he only knew it – but he is unperturbed. He naively trusts Catesby to report to him on the outcome of the council meeting from which he and Stanley must perforce be absent (ll. 20–2). His absolute confidence in his own interpretation of Stanley's dream and his scoffing of the 'mock'ry of unquiet slumbers' (l. 25) enhance the image of his colossal complacency. Wrapped in the arms of Mistress Shore, Hastings is a stranger to 'unquiet slumbers' and has no time for their terrifying contents.

33–93 Catesby enters as Stanley's Messenger exits: do their paths cross? Does Catesby recognize him as Stanley's man and wonder, with the secret informer's sixth sense, what can have been so urgent for Stanley to rouse Hastings so early in the morning? He wastes no time in sounding Hastings out (ll. 37–8). Tired and perhaps a little irritable, Hastings queries Catesby's quasi-euphemistic 'wear the garland': Why can't people say what they mean? Hastings is unequivocally against Richard's ascent and in the first of a series of heavy if not overweight ironies, he effectively says 'over my dead body', which is, as we know, an obstacle over which Richard is more than happy to step. News of the imminent killings at Pomfret does much to raise Hastings's spirits, and in this cheery frame of mind he envisages further blood-lettings and score-settlings in the next two weeks: Who will he send packing? Dorset?

It is no wonder Richard and Buckingham admire and trust Catesby: all three share a wicked sense of humour, a wavelength of dry morbidity apparently beyond the frequency ranges of other characters. ''Tis a vile thing to die, my gracious lord, / When men are unprepared and look not for it' (ll. 62–3) is a joke for us and a highly gratuitous taunt for the stubbornly obtuse Hastings, whose response, 'O, monstrous, monstrous' (l. 64), might also get a laugh if uttered with sufficient insincerity. With the aside about Hastings's decapitation, Catesby speaks with his master's voice, as it were; he is the privileged Vice-figure in this scene. Stanley enters, frazzled and haggard after his unquiet night. He is tense and is not revived by Hastings's cajoling (ll. 72–3). By now, the news of events at Pomfret has marinated to such an extent that Hastings can even describe himself as in a 'triumphant' mood – the political state may be tott'ring (l. 35), but his own personal state is 'secure' (l. 80). Stanley is anxious to get to the meeting at the Tower, but Hastings is not ready to leave; here is an opportunity, unauthorized by the text but dramatically rich, for Mistress Shore (or even an anonymous servant) to bring out overcoat and documents from his 'house' and for Hastings to be too busy dressing, etc., to be able to leave with Stanley and Catesby. Might he be arranging his headgear at the moment Stanley grimly comments: 'They for their truth might better wear their heads / Than some that have accused them wear their hats' (ll. 91–2)? Might Stanley's lines be an aside, either to himself or to Catesby? Do we see Catesby instantly registering their pro-Queen sentiments?

94 to the end   A **Pursuivant** – a Royal or state messenger with power to execute warrants – enters; not the kind of figure Stanley, fearing the boar's machinations, is glad to see and he exits quickly. Hastings, on the contrary, knows the man, who curiously, in Q at least, shares his name (l. 95). As in the closing moments of *The Comedy of Errors* when the twin Dromios get re-acquainted, two men with the same name are alone on stage together. What is Shakespeare up to here? Although he would have found the coincidence of names in his sources, he could easily have changed that of the cameo character. Perhaps lurking in the background is the old belief that meeting one's *doppelgänger* (here conceived as someone with the same name) is a sure prelude to death. But then again, they have already met; perhaps it was even Hastings the Pursuivant who arrested Hastings the politician and forced the latter to go 'prisoner to the Tower' (l. 99). The Pursuivant makes little contribution beyond a series of short, sycophantic remarks and figurative tugs of his forelock; it is Hastings's remarkable, apparently ever-growing light-headedness that dominates this unit of the scene. He gives (Q) or throws (F) his purse to the Pursuivant, and, in F, specifies that its contents should be converted into booze. A **priest** enters, apparently overhearing the Pursuivant's closing wish that 'God save your lordship' (l. 106). To our relief, he is not called Hastings but Sir John. It is unclear what exactly Hastings might whisper in the priest's ear – if previous form is anything to go by, he's confessing his excitement at the Pomfret slaughter. Whatever the content, it is an unlikely sight that greets the entering

Buckingham. The scene closes with another sardonic aside (l. 118), affirming the dramaturgical kinship between Buckingham, Catesby and Richard. It is not hard to imagine Hastings whistling as he goes off to work.

Act III, scene iii

1 to the end   We have heard so much of Pomfret over the last few minutes that it seems logical that this scene should briefly transport us there. Rivers, Grey and **Vaughan** enter as prisoners, their chances of escape so slim that they need only one **guard**. Perhaps they are manacled to each other; perhaps, too, the guard scans them with a gun. The director might have chosen to add Vaughan to earlier court scenes to avoid the confusion of his appearance now, although Shakespeare, in Q at least, did not find the role interesting enough to enrich it with lines in this scene. In Clarence's execution scene, we have observed the perils of working with amateur assassins. Here we see the slick professionalism of the state as embodied in the grimly business-like **Sir Richard Ratcliffe**. In Act I, scene iii we learn that 'Talkers are no good doers' – whatever else Ratcliffe may be, he is not a talker.

Although Vaughan is silent, Rivers and Grey seem determined not to go quietly into the dark night of death. Their speeches not only emphasize their innocence but also function to evoke the whole sweep of history – from Richard II's murder, via the Battle of Tewkesbury, and Margaret's ritual cursing in Act I, scene iii – that has led to this moment. There is some distinction between their tones: Rivers unequivocally protests (too much?) their innocence (l. 12), but Grey offers the appropriately shaded realization that they are culpable of standing by when Richard stabbed Margaret's son, Prince Edward (ll. 13–14). Ratcliffe is weary with the indignant apostrophes to God for revenge, and with a bureaucrat's sense of urgency calls time: 'Come, come despatch. The limit of your lives is out' (l. 21). The three captives embrace – perhaps we remember the group embrace of Elizabeth, the Duchess and Clarence's children in Act II, scene ii, a visual motif for Richard's victims. Although Shakespeare has kept his depiction of onstage violence in *Richard III* noticeably chaste, the director may still decide to end this scene at Pomfret with a fore-shadowing of decapitation. The lights may fade on the lifting of an axe.

Act III, scene iv

Entry A large table and set of chairs are brought on to prepare the stage for one of Shakespeare's greatest representations of power politics. In F, Buckingham, Hastings, Stanley and the Bishop of Ely are joined by Norfolk, Ratcliffe, Lovell and the now familiar '*others*'. Q stipulates only 'the lords' and, given that only four men speak, it is possible (as Jowett's edition maintains) that only these men are present. Q thus not only avoids the awkward re-entrance of Ratcliffe (whom we have just seen despatching the prisoners a few hundred miles north of the Tower), but heightens the impression that we are now at the hard core, the inner sanctum of national politics. The fate of the nation is in these hands. But where is Richard? Typically, Shakespeare creates anticipation through absence.

1–22 Hastings, still riding the crest of Act III, scene ii, is keen to get down to business. The main if not only item on the agenda is to agree on a date for the coronation of Prince Edward. As we will soon learn, at this point Catesby has not yet reported back to Buckingham. He is therefore unaware that Hastings (and therefore Stanley) is opposed to Richard's usurpation of the throne. His first question (l. 4) provides either with a chance to stall the rush towards the coronation. The gambit fails – Buckingham is apparently surrounded by loyalists to the old king and the heir presumptive. His only tactic left is to invoke the intentions of Richard, the Lord Protector. 'Who knows the Lord Protector's mind herein?' (l. 7) is a veiled invitation to Hastings: Are you with us or against us? Ely rightly points out that Buckingham seems Richard's closest ally, but Buckingham suavely deflects this by explicitly inviting Hastings to reflect on his relationship with Richard. Hastings, of course, is blind to this, and even presumes to speak on Richard's behalf, a move that – in keeping with the dramaturgical logic of the play – prompts Richard's entrance. An echo, an inversion and an irony: like Hastings in Act III, scene ii,

Richard enters as if fresh from bed (perhaps he is still arranging his garments?); unlike Hastings, he has overslept, the irony of which will be thrown into relief by Anne's later claim that her husband suffered terrible 'timorous dreams' (IV.i.80) and by Richard's onstage nightmare on the eve of the Battle of Bosworth. Of course, it is likely that he has been up for hours, but Richard's choice of excuse is revealing: heavy sleepers have clean consciences and are not generally on the verge of a *coup d'état*. Buckingham makes a faux slip (l. 29) – is he trying to alert Richard to Hastings's opposition to their cause?

23–63   Richard is in a jaunty, whimsical mood. The request for the Bishop of Ely to send for strawberries is as bizarre as the director wants it to be. The men are gathered to determine nothing less than the future King of England's succession and all Richard can think about is fruit. The Bishop might well be baffled to receive such an incongruous injunction. As Richard leaves, he takes Buckingham aside, presumably downstage towards us, their co-conspirators. If Jowett's interpretation of Q is followed, this creates the rather striking image of Hastings and Stanley – the loyalists – marooned and bewildered at the table. Richard confirms what we already knew and what Buckingham was surely coming to suspect: Hastings's head must be detached from his body if Richard is to be King. In a move that can only appear sinister to Stanley – for whom the nightmarish memory of the boar is still fresh – Richard and Buckingham, for no apparent reason, quit the stage. Stanley fills the awkward void left by their departure with an attempt to return to the agenda. The Bishop returns – 'I have sent for these strawberries' probably means that he has sent someone to fetch them, but it is much more dramatically interesting – if logistically improbable – that he has them in his hands. Actors prefer not to work with children or animals, but fruit or indeed food of any kind is another matter. The Bishop's half-line (l. 52) strongly implies a brief hiatus. Hastings's attempt to fill the void marks the moment when irony shades into idiocy. So many people, from the Third Citizen to his own mother, have commented on Richard's inherent untrustworthiness that for Hastings now to offer an encomium to his transparency seems to be pushing the bounds of psychological credibility. A more charitable reading might find the actor delivering the lines with a deep sense of unease, as if it were an exercise in wishful thinking. Stanley's responses are notably circumspect (ll. 59–60, 63).

63–83 Richard and Buckingham re-enter. Richard's mood has inexplicably altered from the cheerful and smooth to the furious paranoia of the persecuted. Even now, though, Hastings may still feel secure – this might all be a ruse to justify the execution of the Queen's kinsmen at Pomfret. Hastings affirms, probably after an uneasy silence, that traitors deserve death, and Richard's excitement mounts. He makes a spectacle of himself, perhaps rolling up his sleeve to reveal his arm fully for what might be the first time. The extent of the arm's withered deformity will depend on the effect the director seeks to make at this juncture. While this is an obvious invitation to the make-up department and the actor to shock, it might also be dramatically effective if there is nothing visibly wrong with the limb; an absence of deformity would underline the trumped-up, fictive nature of Richard's accusations. The naming of 'Edward's wife' (l. 75) as responsible surely surprises no one, but the immediate conjunction with Mistress Shore turns all eyes on Hastings. He is now directly implicated in the witchcraft and is suddenly thrust into the impossible position of having to condemn or defend his lover. No fan of due process when it came to the deaths of the Queen's faction at Pomfret, he now begins to invoke the principle of innocence before proven guilt:

> If they have done this thing, my gracious lord –
>
> (l. 78)

And that is enough. Jowett, following More's account of this moment, has Richard '*clap his fist on the table*', presumably the same arm that formed Exhibit A in his charge of witchcraft. While Jowett's suggestion is more than plausible, there is nevertheless the possibility that the word 'traitor' is the prearranged cue for Catesby and the soldiers to enter. (On the personnel variants between Q and F here, see Jowett's note to line 80.I.) It is at this highly dramatic moment that the Bishop's strawberries – if on stage – might come into play.

An off-hand Richard might nonchalantly consider their consumption, only to check himself with the resolution that he 'will not dine today' until he has seen Hastings' severed head (ll. 82–3). A more engaged, if not psychotic Richard might, for example, smear the strawberries over Hastings's face in a prefiguration of blood-letting and an echo, for those who are seeing this *Richard III* in the context of the first tetralogy, of Margaret's smearing of his father's face with the blood of Young Rutland (*3 Henry VI*, I.iv.80–4).

84 to the end   In a moment depressingly familiar from accounts of dictators of every age, Richard capitalizes on the general fear instilled by the victimization of Hastings to demand the loyalty of all: 'The rest that love me, come and follow me' (l. 84). What will Stanley and Ely do? Will either be brave enough to protest against the absurd brutality of what they have just witnessed? Assuming that Richard leaves the stage first, does Buckingham follow immediately in his wake or does he pause, intensifying the pressure on Ely and Stanley to nail their colours to the mast? Faced with the unenviable choice between moral compromise and death, both choose the former, taking their leave of Hastings in silence.

Hastings laments both his obtuseness and his *schadenfreude*, his recent delight in his enemies' misfortune. If, as in Q, he is left alone with Catesby and an unspecified number of soldiers, this speech could either be addressed to himself as one thinking aloud, as it were, or might be delivered to Catesby, a man whom Hastings might still see as a sympathetic friend. Such an illusion would not last long. Catesby's terse, ice-cold interruption (ll. 99–100) both echoes the business-like register of Ratcliffe (to whom this speech is attributed in F) at Pomfret, and completes Catesby's sinister role in Hastings's tragedy. Hastings's conventional summation of the vanity of worldly things seems to elicit a smirk from the impatient henchman: 'They smile at me that shortly shall be dead' (l. 108).

Act III, scene v

1–18   The next scene may open with the sound of laughter, as if to envelop Richard and Buckingham too within Hastings's closing prognosis. The chase for the crown is becoming thrilling and, with Hastings now disposed of and the other power-brokers in a state of fearful acquiescence, the mighty dukes are closing in on their target. They enter here in '*rotten armour, marvellous ill-favoured*', that is, in theatrical rather than functional military gear. The impression that these are ad-libbed costumes is substantiated by the conversation's theme of acting and pretence. The delivery of these lines mimics the subject. Richard simultaneously describes and performs the actorly trick of murdering his breath in the middle of a word ('And then begin again, [pause] and stop again [pause]'), while Buckingham no doubt 'look[s] back' and pries on every side in the manner of the deep tragedian (ll. 3–7). This hamminess is entertaining, but its point only becomes clear with the arrival of the Lord Mayor. Richard goes berserk and instantly creates the impression that the room is under attack; Buckingham makes what he knows will be a fruitless attempt to convey information to the Mayor (l. 15). Catesby is managing affairs off stage and it is no doubt he who provides the sound effect of an aggressive drum. The cacophony builds only to be defused by the great anti-climax of Catesby's entrance (after l. 18). Perhaps the drum has heralded an execution, as Catesby carries with him (on a pole? in a bag? held by the hair?) the head of Hastings. The actors now have a new prop.

19–70 Richard, as he has already with Clarence and probably with Anne, makes a show of his tears (l. 22). The head might already have been passed to him for inspection by now. The Lord Mayor perhaps reacts squeamishly to the gory locks as Richard has to prompt him to focus his attention – 'Look ye, my lord Mayor' (l. 25). Why this fuss about the Mayor? He is the central focus of Richard's and Buckingham's combined energy. It rapidly becomes clear that their present challenge – the cause of all the hubbub with which the scene began – is to persuade the Mayor of the legitimacy of Hastings's execution. When Buckingham weighs in (ll. 32ff.), there is a strong sense of the dukes' performing a pincer movement of persuasion around the static Mayor. His 'What, had he so?' (l. 39) could be shocked belief, but could also, alternatively, mean 'Pull the other one,' depending on how gullible the actor wants the Mayor to appear.

If the latter reading is adopted, there could be genuine menace in Richard's succeeding speech, a thinly veiled threat that the Mayor should tow the official line or he too might be accused of treason and summarily despatched. Hastings's head here serves as a peculiarly effective *momento mori*. Weighing the situation up, the Mayor, whether sincerely or not, acquiesces in the fiction: 'Now fair befall you!' (l. 46), even comically echoing Richard's earlier allusion to Hastings's affair with Shore (l. 50). Having secured the Mayor's loyalty, Richard administers a mock reprimand to 'these our friends' (gesturing to Catesby) for executing Hastings before the Mayor could hear his confession. At the mention of 'the citizens' (l. 59) we might remember the three representatives of the public we saw in Act II, scene iii – it is this potentially sceptical audience that the Mayor must now convince on Richard's behalf. Until now, Richard's plotting has been directed at the elimination of individuals, but now the public dimension of the race for the crown is foregrounded, preparing us for the crowd scene with which this Act will climax.

70–100   The Mayor exits to persuade the citizens of Richard's 'just proceedings'. He is, in modern political terms, 'on message'. There is no time to celebrate the success of their hypocrisy: Richard completes Buckingham's half-line farewell as the Mayor leaves, and urges further movement (l. 70). His mind is racing as he primes Buckingham with the catalogue of slanders with which he must pollute popular perception (ll. 72–90). The afterthought of concern for his mother's feelings should surely be comic, a shared joke. Buckingham's response, 'I'll play the orator / As if the golden fee for which I plead / Were for myself' (ll. 93–5), could introduce an element of tension. What does Buckingham hope to gain from all this? We know that he is to be rewarded with an enormous estate, but if 'the golden fee' for which Buckingham is about to plead is the Crown of England, might it threaten Richard to hear Buckingham – even subjunctively – imagining this fee as his own, 'for myself'? The seeds of the partnership's future tensions and dissolution could be subtly sown here.

101 to the end   The coda to the scene presents options to the director. If following Q, Richard is left alone with Catesby; or, with some creative latitude, Catesby might exit earlier (either as coercive company for the Mayor or as support for Buckingham), leaving Richard alone with his audience for the final four lines of scheming. If F has been followed, of course, he will be flanked by Lovell and Ratcliffe, whom he instructs to prepare Doctor Shaw and Friar Penker for the ensuing shenanigans at Baynard's Castle, before they exit and he confides to us his plans to sideline Clarence's children and isolate the Princes (ll. 101–4).

Act III, scene vi

1 to the end This short scene packs a punch beyond its length. The **Scrivener**'s soliloquy offers a behind-the-scenes glimpse into the mechanisms of corruption and injustice on which any *coup d'état* depends. If Richard has held the stage alone for the final lines of the preceding scene, he is now replaced by a strongly contrasting solitary figure, a representative of decency and moral outrage. And yet, despite his awareness of his part in the falsification of history, the Scrivener remains an obedient cog in the machine of Richard's progress: he is bold enough to say that he sees 'this palpable device', yet not bold enough to refuse to play his part in it. We are reminded of Brackenbury's wish to be innocent of Clarence's murder by shutting down his moral faculty and blanking out the implications of his complicity (I.iv.85–6). But the Scrivener's speech also has a broader, metatheatrical application to us, his audience. We have also been complicit with Richard, laughing at his jokes, enjoying his savagery, encouraging his canter to the crown – we, like Brackenbury, like the Scrivener, like the Mayor, have failed to resist and remained passive. 'Who's so gross / That cannot see this palpable device?' (ll. 10–11) might be a direct challenge to us, the audience: what are we doing? Or, perhaps more accurately, what *would* we do?

Act III, scene vii

1–40 With Richard and Buckingham entering from opposite sides of the stage (*'at one door . . . at another'*), it is plausible that the Scrivener exits upstage centre, leaving a space briefly charged with moral indignation before the vacuum is filled with the meeting of the amoral partners. Richard's reliance on Buckingham – apparent throughout this scene – is signalled immediately by his informational dependency: 'How now, my lord, what say the citizens?' (l. 1). Buckingham may be a little weary after his oratorical exertions, but the pace of this dialogue must not flag. On the Elizabethan stage there would have been no significant interval; on the modern stage it is most likely an intermission will be placed at the end of this scene. The audience has, therefore, been concentrating for a long time by now, and the actors must drive the play through these final minutes with energy and conviction.

Buckingham's report of his extolling of Richard's virtues may pause for a millisecond to register the strangeness of Richard having resembled his father in his 'form' – a weird and instantly disprovable lie – but, on the whole, the speech (ll. 5–19) requires a crescendo effect, capped by Richard's 'Ah, and did they so?', which must be excited and upwardly inflected, literally high-pitched, for the full flattening force of Buckingham's 'No' (l. 20). It would require effort for the actor not to get a laugh with this monosyllable. Buckingham continues his report with undiminished vigour, now, actor that he is, incorporating impersonations of the Recorder and a handful of planted Citizens into his narrative. The scene appears, briefly, to break down:

> What, tongueless blocks were they? Would they not speak?
> No, by my troth, my lord.
>
> (ll. 37–8)

But the sense of urgency is instantly reignited by the news that 'the Mayor is here at hand' (l. 40) – Buckingham gestures to the wings – and that therefore the real endgame, the final furlong to the crown, is about to be entered. Buckingham's earlier frustrated accounts of his failure to persuade the Citizens have, we now realize, acted as red herrings. The game remains afoot.

41–50 If Q is followed and the lines in F about Doctor Shaw and Friar Penker (after III.iii.100) are cut, then Buckingham's suggestion that Richard 'stand betwixt two churchmen' (l. 43) might effectively place inverted commas round 'churchmen', implying that they will be nothing of the sort. Richard has already suggested this brilliantly hypocritical piece of stage management (III.iii.97–8); Buckingham might here offer a modification. (The 'holy descant' (l. 44) may remind us of Richard's earlier image of descanting on his own deformity.) Following the logic of Buckingham's misogynist analogy (l. 46), Richard must now assume a feminized, passive persona, while Buckingham has cast himself as the aggressive wooer. 'Get you up to the leads' (l. 50) he tells Richard, indicating an area above the playing space – a scaffold, balcony, raised aperture or hydraulic platform, depending on the nature of the theatre and the set designer's budget.

51–77 The Mayor enters with '*Citizens*'. Once again, the director will have to decide on the nature of this crowd. Catesby later refers to 'Such troops of citizens' (l. 80), so, if this description is not intentionally ironic, the stage will presumably be filled with as many actors as the company can afford. (Given that this scene will probably be followed by an interval, the actors required in IV.i and IV.ii will have plenty of time to change back into their named character's costume; thus the troop could consist of citizens of both sexes.) According to Buckingham's account, the citizens have so far reacted with marked reluctance to the slanders of Edward and the Princes and the simultaneous puffing of Richard. But perhaps this crowd of citizens contains a disproportionately high percentage of Buckingham's 'followers' (l. 30), the 'ten voices' or so who responded obediently by crying 'God save King Richard!' (l. 32). On the other hand, it might also contain the three Citizens we have met in Act II, scene iii, and we know them to be not entirely sure of the desirability of any of the major candidates for the throne. The Mayor, at least, appears to be already convinced of the justice of Richard's claim: 'Marry, God forbid his grace should say us nay' (l. 76) – we know, of course, that 'no' is exactly what Richard will appear to say, and the remainder of the scene will explore how far Richard can push this show of reticence without blowing his chances entirely.

78–103 Catesby acts as a go-between, shuttling back and forth from Buckingham to the offstage Richard. He might be placed on the

upper playing area from his first entrance (after l. 52), or could enter
at floor level at first, then reappear above on his second entrance
(after l. 77). Catesby and Buckingham's double act is wonderfully
slick, providing the perfect build-up to Richard's appearance – an
appearance which, like the entrances in I.iii, II.i and III.iv,
Shakespeare delays to maximize the impact of Richard's stage presence. The question of mood is vital in this scene and will depend
much on the characterization of the Mayor and the citizens. Clearly
the Mayor will never be the most perceptive of characters, but if the
actor pushes him towards buffoonery the scene will gain opportunities for comedy while necessarily sacrificing tension. For example,
how convincing are these 'two bishops' between whom Richard
stands? A burlesque production would pick up on Buckingham's
'churchmen' and make it obvious that these are a couple of Richard's
lackeys (Ratcliffe and Lovell being the obvious choices if the Folio
text is being followed) who have rapidly thrown on some cassocks,
have no idea how to cross themselves, hold their Bibles the wrong
way up, and generally reek more of the pub than the pulpit. Yet such
old vaudevillian tricks could detract from the tension of the scene –
it might also be a good deal more sinister if these are *real* clergymen,
symptoms of how far Richard's tentacles reach through the rotten
body politic. The prayer book Richard holds in his hand might have
been tossed to him by Buckingham (see l. 42); the short stretch of
action between lines 50 and 89 also give him the opportunity for a
rudimentary costume change, possibly into a loose-fitting monastic
robe, at least, and – if wanted – a pair of devout spectacles.

104–202   One of the dramaturgical challenges of this scene
concerns Buckingham's positioning. With Richard behind and above
him, the actor must 'cheat' (a theatrical term for when an actor,
contradicting the laws of natural behaviour, adjusts his body towards
the audience and away from the person he is talking to). If he consistently addresses Richard directly, he will up-stage himself, and possibly will not be heard clearly by the audience. The most fruitful option
for Buckingham here is to address the theatre audience as if we too
were citizens of London. Not only does this offer a practical solution
to a spatial and acoustic quandary, it also intensifies our sense of

involvement – and complicity – in Richard's rise. Buckingham's rhetoric (ll. 112–33) is grand, over-blown, the declamatory speech of a king-maker. Richard, in keeping with their prearranged contrast between bold wooer and reticent maiden, adopts a much quieter, rather elegantly phrased humility (ll. 134–56). It is time for Buckingham to up the ante, which he does with his increasingly animated and bitter account of Prince Edward's bastardy (ll. 157–83). Does he physically or figuratively nudge the Mayor here, prompting his brief shout of encouragement, echoed by Catesby (ll. 184–5)? Richard again unequivocally blocks their entreaties and there may be a submerged sense in Buckingham's next speech that he had not expected Richard to drag this tango of deceit out for so long. If so, the exit ('Come, citizens. Zounds, I'll entreat no more', l. 201) might be a coded message to Richard to strike when the iron is next hot. Richard seems to be enjoying his role – it's the last time we'll see his mock-pious act and perhaps he knows it; only someone completely in character could come out with the brilliant improvised response: 'Oh do not swear, my lord of Buckingham' (l. 202).

203 to the end At least one citizen remains behind and does not follow Buckingham off. Perhaps by this point, a pro-Richard faction has clearly emerged among the 'troop' and it is this cluster that has been loath to give up so easily. Is it the naturally optimistic Second Citizen of Act II, scene iii, who appeals directly to Richard at line 204? The martyred, plaintive tone of 'Would you enforce me to a world of care?' is immediately undercut by the pragmatic 'Well, call them again' (ll. 205–6). When the stage is once more full after Buckingham's and the citizens' re-entry, Richard finally – and with a sly allusion to his deformity (ll. 210–11) – accepts the crown. Buckingham's job is done now he is able to cry 'Long live Richard, England's royal king!' (l. 222). Q follows this with the Mayor's under-whelming 'Amen', but in performance it will be hard to avoid the temptation to follow F and let the citizens echo Buckingham's bless-ing. Interestingly, Shakespeare has not supplied the obvious 'bang' at the very close of this scene. There is no rhyming couplet; no moment of Richard alone, sharing his glee with the audience; no clear piece of business that might trap a clap for the new King. Instead, we have the rather downbeat promise of the return to 'our holy task', and the farewells to Buckingham and 'gentle friends' (ll. 227–8). We are now almost exactly two-thirds of the way through the play, Richard has reached his zenith, at the height of Fortune's wheel, and the audience wants an interval. Under such circumstances, any creative, non-textual climax that provides a strong curtain seems not only permissible but desirable.

ACT IV

Act IV, scene i

1–51 The last time we saw the Queen, the Duchess of York and Dorset, the women were on the verge of seeking sanctuary; the last (and only) time we have seen Anne was way back in Act I, scene ii when she succumbed to Richard's seduction. The two parties here enter from opposite sides of the stage, initiating a scene which, after our long exposure to the main plot of Richard's quest for the crown, will help balance our pleasure at his rise with an awareness and concern for his victims. The opening line, 'Who meets us here?' is not only a conventional marker of the space between the Duchess and Anne; it might also imply that Anne's appearance has changed dramatically since we last saw her. As she will soon tell us, her married life has been scarred by misery and insomnia. She has not managed one hour's consecutive sleep and her bearing should correspond, with that hollowed-out, ghostly quality typical of chronic insomniacs. The Queen and Dorset have, of course, also suffered in the interim: we can assume that they have by now heard of the executions at Pomfret. But, unlike us, they are ignorant of Richard's *coup* and still expect the imminent coronation of Prince Edward, and their mood of excited anticipation could form a contrast to Anne's weariness.

Our sense of location is quickly established with the mention of the Tower (l. 3). Brackenbury enters, as if from the Tower, and bars entrance with a terrific Freudian slip: 'The King hath strictly charged the contrary' (l. 12). Just as this unit of the scene reaches a literal impasse with Brackenbury's final denial and exit, Stanley enters – it never rains but it pours. His greeting (ll. 24–6) is elliptical, hinting that he finds his news difficult to break. His auditors' puzzlement prompts the more direct, unequivocal address to Anne – she is now the Queen in all but title. News of the imminent coronation causes something of a seizure in Elizabeth. Barred access to her younger sons, her first thought now is for the one son she can save; her advice that Dorset flee to join Richmond in France is vital in initiating our sense of a counter-movement against Richard. It is hours since we first heard the name 'Richmond'. Then it was the Queen, again, reprimanding Stanley for the alleged plotting of his wife, 'The Countess Richmond' (I.iii.20). Now the name is reinvented to bear positive connotations. Stanley reminds us that Richmond is his (step-)son (l. 45), thus also alerting us to his forthcoming role in the resistance movement against King Richard.

52 to the end   Stanley stresses the urgency of his embassage (l. 52), but Anne resists this appeal; every fibre of her being wants to delay the inevitable exit to Westminster. Her lines (ll. 54–8) imagine a violent assisted suicide: the death-wish implicit in her decision to marry Richard is here made explicit and the actor might choose to make 'Anointed let me be with deadly poison' (l. 57) a statement of intent, as if to say, 'my only way out of this is to kill myself'. As often in *Richard III* and the first tetralogy in general, the memory of a previous pivotal event is rehearsed and quoted in grim hindsight. Although we cannot know it for sure, this is Anne's death speech. Like Hastings and the lords at Pomfret before her, she considers her innocence, her gullibility and the potency of curses. One of the few people on whom Margaret did not lay a curse in Act I, scene iii, she has damned herself. Following the evocative portrait of her turbulent marriage bed (ll. 78–80), she states her position with blank, brutal realism: 'Besides, he hates me for my father Warwick / And will, no doubt, shortly be rid of me' (ll. 81–2). If the director does not choose to bring her on in the following scene, the audience should be left in no doubt that this is the last time we will see Anne.

The Duchess of York takes organizational control, dispersing the characters in several directions. If F is followed, the scene concludes not with the Duchess's weary resolve to exit to her grave (a red herring: we will see her again), but with Elizabeth's apostrophe to the Tower, an important and ominous reminder to the audience that the Princes still live.

Act IV, scene ii

Entry   As with the transition between I.iv (Clarence's murder) and II.i, a scene of private suffering in or near the Tower is followed by the sound of trumpets and the entry of the court. If Edward sat on a throne in II.i, we now see the same property ready for a new occupant. According to the stage direction, Richard enters already crowned, but the director might decide that the actual act of coronation should take place at the beginning of this scene as a dumbshow underscored by ceremonial music. Once again, Shakespeare is permissive about the personnel present. Buckingham, Catesby and a **Boy** are required by Q, with F adding Ratcliffe and Lovell. 'Other nobles' leaves it up to the director to decide how densely populated this scene should be. It seems probable that such figures as the Lord Mayor and the Bishop of Ely will be present to symbolize the state's ratification of Richard's new reign. Anne has sufficient time since her exit in IV.i (especially if Elizabeth's F-only closing speech on the Princes is retained) to re-enter and become a reluctant participant in the coronation. If the coronation is staged, we might see Anne herself crowned: does she feel the golden metal as if it were indeed 'red-hot steel' (IV.i.55–6)? Equally, the opening lines and action of the scene – in which Richard asks that Buckingham give him his hand, perhaps to lead him to the throne – offer the spectacle of an infernal marriage between the two dukes that has easily eclipsed that between Richard and Anne. Anne's absence is signalled by the centrality of the man who appears to own the lion's share of Richard's affection.

1–44   For the first time, we hear the compound 'King Richard' (l. 3) from the man himself. He is richly dressed. A score or two of tailors, presumably, have worked on the coronation outfit. For whatever complex of reasons – spite, compensation, lust for power for power's sake – Richard has dreamt of this moment of ascension and accession

for years. But what is the substance of kingship? What are its benefits? Having hacked his way through the thorny wood and waded
over pools of now-congealed blood, what is it that awaited Richard
on the other side? This scene shows us. Richard II, in Shakespeare's
later play of that name, describes Death as allowing each King 'a
breath, a little scene / To monarchize, be feared, and kill with looks,
/ Infusing him with self and vain conceit' (III.ii.160–2) before coming
at the last to claim his life. Richard Gloucester's peremptory style of
monarchizing is immediately apparent in his demand that all the
court save Buckingham keep their distance from him: 'Stand all
apart' (l. 1). In such commands and the many others like them that
will ensue, the actor will show how much King Richard relishes his
newly-sanctified power over the bodies of others. But the worm in
the bud of kingship is almost immediately revealed in Richard's
dialogue with Buckingham. (With the rest of the court presumably
arranged at some distance from the throne, perhaps lining the
margins of the stage, we accept the convention that this dialogue is
an extended aside and out of general earshot.) Already we are
presented with a strong pictorial image of the lonely and isolated
quality of Richard's power and this is further emphasized by the
incipient rift in their relationship that Buckingham and Richard's
interchange reveals.

Until now, Buckingham has been Richard's 'second self', their
partnership based on mutual understanding and perfectly attuned
wavelengths of thought. Now Richard's nervous energy appears to
pour into a non-conductor. Buckingham's failure to 'Think now
what I would say' (l. 9) throughout this dialogue offers the actor an
option: either he knows exactly what Richard is getting at and feigns
incomprehension, or he might be genuinely confused by the elliptical quality of Richard's statements, his doubt only resolved with the
indelicate frankness of 'I wish the bastards dead' (l. 17). 'Give me some
breath, some little pause' (l. 23) – a striking anticipation of Richard II's
characterization of kingship quoted above – sounds like a man with
whom conscience is meddling, just as it did with the Second
Executioner. Buckingham's exit leaves Richard utterly isolated in the
centre of the stage. Unselfconsciously he bites his lip, an action
which Catesby decodes (l. 26) – the actor might choose to make this

a habit and use it to convey anger and frustration throughout the performance. Richard decides to act without Buckingham's assent, an ominous shift for the man who is now off stage, pondering his next move. The boy who recommends Tyrrell to Richard might well be played by one of the actors seen previously as either of the Princes and/or Clarence's children; even if not, that a young male is a key accessory to the Princes' murder is a clear irony that will not be lost on the audience. The boy's claim that 'Gold were as good as twenty orators' (l. 37) in persuading Tyrrell to commit murder is another echo: we remember that Buckingham has previously played the orator for a golden fee; he will now be replaced by an unthinking man of action not words. The substitution is confirmed in Richard's aside (ll. 41–4).

45–65   Stanley enters to deliver the news of Dorset fleeing to join Richmond. 'I hear' presents the information as second-hand, even a rumour, whereas we know that Stanley himself has been instrumental in engineering the desertion. Richard does not verbally respond to the mention of Richmond's name, but perhaps he impatiently waves Stanley away in the empty second half of Stanley's line (l. 47). The logic of the space seems to dictate that there is only ever room for one courtier next to the throne, and as Stanley retreats, Catesby takes his place. Although Jowett has the whole speech (ll. 50–9) as an aside to Catesby, the actor might choose to make 'Anne my wife is sick and like to die' (either at line 51 and/or at line 57) a louder statement, obviously intended as a practical attempt to start the rumour-mongering. If Anne is indeed on stage throughout this scene, there are clear possibilities here for callous sadism and public humiliation. Like Buckingham minutes before, Catesby seems to suffer from qualms – 'Look how thou dream'st!' (l. 56). Alone again, Richard (as in lines 41–5) explains to the audience his course of action. While this recalls to us the Vice-like Richard of the play's earlier Acts, the tone is now almost entirely different. There may be a vestigial trace of the entertaining dark humorist in 'Murder her brothers, and then marry her. Uncertain way of gain' (ll. 62–3), but Richard's overall mood is neurotic, joyless, a slave to the remorseless momentum of sin plucking on sin. After Buckingham and Catesby's hesitations, he feels the need to remind us and perhaps reassure himself that 'Tear-falling pity dwells not in this eye' (l. 65).

66 to the end   The boy has found **Tyrrell**. The boy has described him as a gentleman with 'humble means' and a 'haughty mind' (ll. 35–6). He has seen better days and needs money if he is to see them again. Unlike Buckingham, he seems to know telepathically what Richard desires (ll. 70–1) and his no-nonsense response (ll. 75–6) lifts Richard's spirits.

Buckingham re-enters; while off stage he has 'considered in [his] mind' Richard's demand that the Princes be killed, but the result of his consideration is swatted aside by Richard ('Well, let that pass') and will not be explicitly revealed. There is a choice here for the actor: has Buckingham completely shaken off his former qualms and resolved to assist in the infanticide (in which case we see the 'old' smooth Buckingham)? Or is he still ambivalent, an ambivalence that can only be cured by the delivery of his promised fee, the earldom of Hereford (in which case we see a more edgy, tentative character)? If, as seems likely, the Quarto text is based on a revised, later version of the play than that on which the Folio is based, it is striking that in lines 99–118 we have the only passage Shakespeare *added* when revising the play. In performance, it is not hard to see why he decided that the melt-down of the relationship between Richard and Buckingham deserved a minute or so more playing time. It is possible that Richard spends most of this scene positioned on the throne – a marked contrast to his earlier energetic bustling and a possible irony: the attainment of kingship and power, by removing all obstacles to desire, paralyses the will and saps energy. To aspire to power is invigorating; to achieve it, exhausting. During the 'clock' passage, however, it might be that Richard's distracted musings on Richmond lead to move-ment. Buckingham's harried interjections might thus be comple-mented by a physical pursuit. It is not clear whether Richard's preoccupation with Richmond is genuine or a performance which spitefully reveals to Buckingham his new, superfluous status – perhaps a mixture of both. Despite his apparent obliviousness, Richard has already decided on the comparison between Buckingham and a 'jack' – the mechanized toy figure that struck the hour on the clock bell – when he finally pays attention to Buckingham with the question 'What's a clock?' (l. 109). It is up to the actor playing Richard to decide whether his final two lines to Buckingham – the last time we will see them together on stage – are icily aloof or fierily angry or move from one to the other. The threat, the sense of 'deep contempt' (l. 122), is clear and Richard exits followed by all except Buckingham, an exit which will on some level visually echo that in Act III, scene iv when Richard, leaving Hastings to his doom, invites 'the rest that love me, come and follow me' (III, iv.84). The message is clear to Buckingham: he, too, thinks on Hastings and promptly resolves to flee, presumably exiting in the opposite direction to that in which the court has just left.

Act IV, scene iii

1–21 The new loyalist replaces the old. If the throne remains on stage for this scene, it will be clear that Tyrrell, his mission accomplished, has returned to the throne-room to seek his employer. There has been little or no hint in the previous scene of the man we now see before us. He seems to be in a state of shock and, typically of the guilt-ridden, he needs to offer a confession. The functional language of his previous exchange with Richard is replaced by a loftier register in the opening lines. The lyrical pathos is heightened further in the reported speeches of Dighton and Forrest, 'fleshed villains' who are distinctly well-spoken and adept in poetic conceits. Shakespeare is, of course, somewhat heavy-handedly seeking to manipulate our emotions here, and there is a clear discrepancy between the 'innocent, alabaster' sleeping princes and the pair we have actually seen on stage. (Perhaps, to paraphrase *Macbeth*, nothing became the Princes' lives like their leaving of them.) In performing the murderers' shocked reactions to their deed, Tyrrell cannot help but be similarly affected; we soon learn that, although he was not present at the infanticide, he has seen the children's corpses (l. 28) and the memory must be fresh in his mind as he speaks to us now.

22–35 At the mention of 'the bloody King' (l. 22), Richard enters. We might hope that Tyrrell's display of remorse might carry over and lead to a direct rebuke to Richard, but, as elsewhere in the play, the fear inspired by tyranny overcomes the individual's instinct to rebel. Tyrrell cannot bring himself to name the deed ('the *thing* you gave in charge', l. 25), before fulfilling Richard's earlier wish that he say 'it is done' (IV.ii.79). Whilst failing in any way to stand up to Richard, Tyrrell keeps his answers plain and mostly short – his exit is notably silent. It is possible that the plainness of his answers is mitigated for Richard by the exchange of a prop: perhaps Tyrrell has with him some item – a recognizable fragment of one of the Princes' costumes? a toy? – which he now presents to Richard as proof of the deed. When Richard requests that he visit him 'at after-supper' and 'tell the process of their death' (l. 32), we know that Tyrrell has no stomach for such a narrative.

If the throne has remained on stage for this scene, Richard may now be seated in it. A brief word about this and other props: in addition to the obvious need for actors to establish relationships with each other in performance, there is also an imperative to define attitudes between actors and props, people and things. The throne and the crown are the two most conventional symbols of kingship and, as such, have been permanent coordinates in Richard's landscape of desire. The actor must, therefore, always seek to discover and then reveal the character's shifting attitudes to these highly charged symbolic objects. How does Richard relate to the throne now that he is King? Is there still a thrill inherent in the object? Is the everyday action of sitting transformed into a moment of supreme arousal? Does the cushion feel luxurious, the arm-rests reassuringly smooth to the touch? Or has it somehow already lost its novelty? Does Richard suffer a demystification? Does his arse stubbornly refuse to feel the difference between this chair and any other? Likewise, is the new crown now oppressive – the mystical totem he always thought would make him tall, powerful, straight – is the weight of this crown now curving his spine and buckling his already crooked legs? Richard does not tell us explicitly. Shakespeare has not given him those lines, but the actor can speak them through his body.

36 to the end   So, here we are alone once again with Richard. Whether he is standing on an empty stage as he did at the play's

opening, or is slumped in the throne, or, alternatively, feeling its
revivifying power is up to the actor and director to decide. The
Princes are dead and, as he informs us, Clarence's children have effectively been debarred from making claims to the throne (ll. 36–7).
Most chillingly, he tells us 'Anne my wife hath bid the world good-
night' (l. 39), a choice of euphemism that reminds the audience of the
insomniac phantasmagoria that was her brief married life. We do not
know how she died, but a natural cause seems unlikely. The mind
that might be comforted by these events obsessively returns to
Richmond. The reference to the crown (l. 42) is troubled: Richard
must now accept that it is a potential object of desire for another and
will therefore never afford him security. He must revive an earlier
role and go to Elizabeth's daughter as 'a jolly thriving wooer' (l. 43).
His momentum is arrested by the 'blunt' and unannounced arrival of
Catesby (rare for this play, in which characters are often invoked and
thus anticipated before entering). Richard's response to Catesby's bad
news equates delay with impotence (l. 53) and the drama picks up
urgency with the resounding couplet and resolute exit with which
the scene ends.

Act IV, scene iv

1–8   Which makes it all the more curious that Shakespeare should
now follow this upbeat urgency with the play's longest and generally
most static scene. Just under a third of the scene (in itself more than
twice the length of the scene that preceded it) is occupied with the
suffering of women; over a third consists of Richard's encounter with
Elizabeth, in which he attempts to woo, by proxy, her daughter.
Directors have frequently worried about the recapitulative nature of
both sections. The first dwells on a long chain of historical events,
some not depicted in *Richard III*, and does not significantly advance
the plot, just at the moment it seems to be accelerating; the second
can appear like a tired re-run of the more dynamic wooing of Anne
close to the play's opening. It is here assumed, however, that the
reader–director will want to experience this scene in its entirety as
part of the expression – whether flawed or not – of Shakespeare's
dramatic design.

With the exit of Richard and Catesby to face the traitors who 'brave the field' (IV.iii.57), the throne may or may not be struck from the stage. If it is, its removal signals to the audience that we have left the court and find ourselves in a no-man's-land, the topography of which must be established by the new scene. The entrance of 'old Queen Margaret' (as F has it) alone, combined with her almost imme-diate use of the word 'now' and her choric summation, provide a strong visual and verbal rhyme with the play's opening. Here, once again, we have an outsider lamenting the spirit of the age in seasonal, metaphorical terms. Furthermore, both moments are dramaturgi-cally inductive, as Margaret's theatrical imagery implies (l. 5); she and Richard are both comfortable with addressing the audience, face-on as it were, and encapsulating a mood. We have not seen Margaret since I.iii.303, some hours in real time and a matter of aeons in stage time (cf. Laertes' long-term absence in *Hamlet*). We have, however, frequently heard her name invoked with anguished reference to the curses she administered in Act I, scene iii. Although time cannot have improved her appearance, it is possible that the witnessing of 'the waning of [her] adversaries' (l. 4) has brought her a degree of content-ment, enough at least to relinquish her lurking spectatorship and resolve to return to France.

8–76 'Who comes here?' (l. 8). Elizabeth and the Duchess of York might both be dressed in mourning black. This would make Elizabeth especially, whom Margaret last saw as a 'painted' and presumably brightly dressed Queen, harder to identify. As Jowett suggests, Richard's later inability to recognize his mother 'might suggest that she is at that point wearing a veil' (p. 297n). How raw is Elizabeth's grief? Is it possible that she has only just received the news of her young sons' deaths? If so, she may not have had the leisure to adjust her dress. As importantly, the rawness of the grief will set the pitch for her emotion as she enters. Various editors have conjectured as to the exact moment at which Elizabeth and the Duchess lose the will to stand. Jowett, for example, has them both sit after line 24. But it is plausible that Elizabeth sinks to her knees earlier, with the apos-trophe to God, which climaxes with the heart-rending 'When did thou [surely 'Thou'] sleep when such a deed was done?' (l. 19), and that the Duchess follows her example. Elizabeth's rhetorical question 'O who have any cause to mourn but I?' (l. 28) will not long go unanswered in this type of company. (Again, the audience is reminded of an earlier moment, the grieving competition between Clarence's children, Elizabeth and the Duchess in II.ii.) The Duchess's response offers a clue to the actor. Her voice should be cracked with woe-weariness (ll. 29–30). Margaret finds the invitation to lament irresistible and reveals herself to them, much as she did to the court in Act I, scene iii. She seeks to unite the women by what they have in common: Richard has killed the men they have bred and/or loved. The Duchess initially rejects this appeal to communion by reminding Margaret of her part in the deaths of York and Rutland, her husband and son (ll. 41–2). Margaret responds with one of the play's most lacerating *ad hominem* attacks, blaming the Duchess for letting loose (l. 49) from the 'kennel of [her] womb . . . A hell-hound that doth hunt us all to death' (l. 45). If Margaret has delivered the invective of lines 43–9 directly to the Duchess – one can imagine her spitting it out at close range – her focus of attention shifts at the end of the speech to God, echoing Elizabeth's apostrophe a minute or so earlier. Does she herself kneel in a parodic allusion to the earlier action? It would certainly make powerful the contrast between her terrible gratitude to the 'upright, just, and true-disposing God' (l. 50) and Elizabeth's reproach to the sleeping, indifferent divinity (ll. 17–19). Margaret recapitulates the tally of losses; short of projecting a genealogical tree on the rear wall of the stage, there is little hope that the audience will confidently distinguish between the numerous Edwards in this account. No matter: the logic is clear. Margaret's loss outweighs all others and the only comfort she can find is in the imminent death of Richard, the last of her curses, which remains unfulfilled.

77–119   If Margaret has so far focused most of her aggressive attention on the Duchess, it is now Elizabeth's turn to feel the heat. Prompted by Elizabeth's recollection of Act I, scene iii, she launches into an expansive memorial reconstruction followed by a schematic inventory of the decline in the former Queen's fortunes (ll. 77–109). Why doesn't Elizabeth interrupt this remorseless summation? It appears that there is no argument to be had and that the answers to the series of questions (ll. 87–91) are so distressingly obvious that there is little point in drawing the breath required to respond. She may have risen on her earlier lines (ll. 74–6) or she might have remained on the ground throughout Margaret's tirade, physically emphasizing both her passivity and her lowliness on Fortune's wheel (cf. l. 99). The onstage energy seems to come exclusively from Margaret; this is her apotheosis and, grimly satisfied, she attempts an exit (after the couplet, ll. 108–9). Before she can leave, Elizabeth – and this seems the most obvious moment for her to rise – stops her and the final exchange between the two allows for a version of female solidarity so far absent from this scene. The two former queens face each other, bereaved and world-weary; might not Margaret's parting advice be intimate, even maternal, a far cry tonally from the melo-drama of her earlier incantations (ll. 70–3)?

120–87 After Margaret's exit – her last of the play – some of her energy seems to have rubbed off on the Duchess and Elizabeth, who now resolve to find Richard and smother him with 'the breath of bitter words' (l. 127). Obligingly, Richard comes to them. After the intensely focused and intimate scene between the three women, the stage is suddenly a chaos of noise and bodies, with drums and trum-pets and men. Do the women physically prevent the passage of Richard's army across the stage or is their mere presence enough to cause the retinue to come to a halt? Richard fails to recognize his own mother, implying either that there is some distance between them or that her face is obscured. When the women list the names of Richard's victims (ll. 137–41), he attempts to drown them out with flourishes and alarums. Intriguingly, he has to demand this twice, opening up the possibility that his musicians fail to respond immedi-ately: are they interested and/or shocked by the women's revelations? Can we assume that Richard's responsibility for many of these deaths is far from being public knowledge and might therefore pique the onlookers' curiosity? Richard and his mother square off, with the son assuming the petulant role of the schoolboy bored by maternal imprecations and in a rush to be somewhere else. (The director will probably not resist the temptation to cut lines 167–8, which are perhaps the most puzzling in the play and hard for the actor to

deliver with any semblance of knowing what they might mean.)
The Duchess's malediction to her son is a vital passage for psycho-
logically-nuanced Richards. Any actor trained in the naturalistic,
post-Stanislavskian approach to character will wonder why it is
that Richard does what he does: what explains the man he is? As
with psychoanalytic critics of the play, the actor's answer might
well be *cherchez la femme*, most obviously the mother who resents
his birth as 'a grievous burden' (l. 160) and seems to have denied
him the nurturing love we (probably more than the Elizabethans)
see as the child's birthright. If the actor does see the Duchess as a
key player in Richard's psyche, then this passage in which she lays
on him her 'most heavy curse' (l. 177) will be devastating. Given that
Richard neither calls for drums and trumpet to drown her out, nor
interrupts her himself, my impression is that he listens intently. In
Act II, scene ii, he has craved her blessing, on his knee, and capped
her pointed wish that God put meekness and love in him with a
cheeky aside to the audience or, plausibly, Buckingham. Here,
following her couplet and exit, words seem to fail him. Only
Elizabeth's coda and attempted exit (ll. 186–7) seem to snap him out
of whatever mental state it is to which his mother's curses have sent
him. The security of the golden crown that he is even now wearing
into warfare depends on his marriage to Elizabeth's daughter. Back
to business.

188–316   The Duchess's exit re-creates a memorable stage image
from earlier in the play. Once again, we see Richard and a female
quarry, backed by an onstage male audience. We cannot but think of
Anne and indeed this long section of Act IV, scene iv, is clearly
intended to form a counterpart to the play's primal wooing scene.
There may not actually be a corpse present on stage over which
Richard must again seduce his victim, but the air is thick with the
memory of the bodies that have stacked up since (ll. 189–90). The
challenge is, if anything, more improbable, the demand more outrageous considering all the bloodied water that has passed under the
bridge between these two characters. In F, the exchange is some 69
lines longer (see Jowett's Appendix A, Passages L and M); Q's shorter,
presumably revised, rendition seems entirely adequate. (Besides, the

Richard actor will be grateful, certainly at the beginning of the run, to have 47 fewer lines to learn.)

Unlike the scene with Lady Anne, this interchange does not involve any obvious use of props. Earlier, corpse, sword and ring provided the actors with focal, dynamic objects with which to express power relations and which made clear staging demands. If Anne's saliva can be considered a biological prop, it, too, carried the implicit direction that Richard should at least be in spitting distance of his assailant. Elizabeth and Richard's exchange, by contrast, is more exclusively a battle of words, a verbal sparring in which their physical relationship (proximity, distance, etc.) is almost entirely open to the actors. Like the earlier dialogue, however, the speech patterns rely heavily on the antitheses and repetitions of stichomythia (ll. 201–7, 264–88) and on split half-lines of instant response and/or interruption (ll. 244–6, 289–98). Again, the ability to lengthen these exchanges, to fall into 'the slower method' Richard aimed for with Anne, endows the character with control of the dialogue and power over the other. Richard's tactic is inevitably to stress the potential of the future rather than the horrors of the past. He offers amnesia as a powerful temptation; he knows that, for this woman, to remember is to suffer. But she, remembering Margaret's advice to dwell on, even exaggerate, the losses of the past, consistently succeeds in invoking brutal history to quash Richard's glamorous visions of 'the time to come'. Thus, the extended stichomythia beginning with Richard's 'Infer fair England's peace by this alliance' (l. 264) is only broken by Elizabeth's response to his outrageous claim that her 'reasons are too shallow and too quick' (l. 282):

> O no, my reasons are too deep and dead:
> Too deep and dead, poor infants, in their grave.
>
> (ll. 283–4)

(It is possible that the second 'too' might be voiced so that we hear 'two'.) The outburst is – as her next line suggests – heart-rending, the effect doubled by the rupturing of the single-line tempo. Richard tries to initiate a longer speech of his own (l. 287) but she successfully dominates the dialogue until line 316. She has obliterated his argument and now seems, like Margaret and the Duchess before her, to be preparing her exit by looking forward to a 'hereafter-time' of solitary grieving in which, to paraphrase Prospero, 'every third thought shall be her grave' (*The Tempest*, V.i.315). It seems plausible to me that the rhyme 'hast/o'erpast' (ll. 315–16), although only a half-rhyme in modern stage Received Pronunciation, indicates the intention to exit, just as couplets did for the women we have recently seen quit the stage for good.

317–49　Why does she not leave at this point? What keeps her on stage and then silent for the duration of Richard's speech (ll. 317–337), a speech she would previously have interrupted? How is Richard's speech sufficiently persuasive to buckle (ostensibly at least) her will and make her even consider being 'tempted of the devil thus' (l. 338)? Elizabeth's behaviour is so enigmatic at her final exit that a range of choices is presented to the actor for how she should react to Richard's pivotal speech. Some critics have concluded (astonishingly, to my mind) that Elizabeth, like Anne before her, is decisively wooed by Richard. The second scene, according to this logic, is a replay of the first – an antagonist is converted into a lover or surrogate wooer – and Richard's verdict that Elizabeth is a 'Relenting fool, and shallow, changing woman' (l. 350) is an accurate summary of what we have just seen. Elizabeth can, of course, be played like that, but this would mean that (a) she somehow finds Richard's speech convincing (is he crying repentant tears again?), and/or (b) she feels an erotic charge towards him, and/or (c) she is genuinely tempted by the notion of being the Queen Mother, restored to the luxuries of the palace. All of which are psychologically plausible – most feelings, however bizarre, can appear plausible. The problem with this reading is that there is absolutely nothing in what Elizabeth says before Richard's speech to support (b) or (c), and it is hard to believe, as (a) demands, that her hitherto mordant scepticism is broken down by his protestation of 'immaculate devotion' (l. 324). Perhaps most importantly, we will soon learn, in the next scene (IV.v.16–17), that Elizabeth has given her daughter to Richmond. The letter that Elizabeth instructs Richard to write her will go unanswered.

An alternative reading to the 'shallow, changing woman' would thus emphasize Elizabeth's canniness: in effect, her ability to deceive – a nice irony given that it is the actor's gift of dissimulation that has served Richard so well earlier in the play. If she fails to exit after line 316, is it because her way is physically barred by Richard? Indeed, might Richard play the entire speech not only as a threat of the consequences of civil war, but, more pointedly, as a direct threat to Elizabeth's body? She is, after all, in heated debate with a psychopath and surrounded by soldiers, any of whom (if Tyrrell is anything to go by) will follow Richard's commands even if they know them to be damnable. Such a reading shifts the emphasis from Richard's seductive powers and Elizabeth's weakness, towards a dynamic of entrapment and escape. She must say something to appease him or she may not leave the stage alive. Played this way, the kiss is suffered rather than in any sense relished, and Richard's grotesque lines on the young Elizabeth's 'nest of spicery' (l. 344) are, especially if reinforced by touch, a form of surrogate rape.

350–415   Does Richard think he has won? For whose benefit does he say 'Relenting fool, and shallow, changing woman' when Elizabeth has exited? For the soldiers and Catesby, who have been on stage throughout the exchange? If so, do they laddishly cheer him on, or is their response more muted, implicitly sympathetic to their former Queen? Or is it a public utterance of another kind, aimed at us in the audience, a pale imitation of 'Was ever woman in this humour wooed'? Is he bullying us to agree with him? If so, we have come a long way from the ease with which he seduced us in the play's opening Act. Finally, might the statement be an attempt to persuade himself that he has triumphed? In the wake of his utter rejection by his mother and his failure to reprise successfully the role of unlikely Lothario, does he reassure himself with a piece of easy misogyny? The subsequent interchanges with Ratcliffe and Catesby (ll. 351–73), in which Richard appropriately suffers the bouts of amnesia he had wished on Elizabeth, imply the early stages of mental disintegration. He is not acting like a commander-in-chief.

Richmond's forces are stirring on all sides. Stanley enters with news of the burgeoning coalition between Dorset, Buckingham, Ely and Richmond. If the throne is still on stage, it should clearly be gestured towards, if not possessively occupied, on Richard's brilliantly sardonic quip 'Is the chair empty?' (l. 387). Like a jealous lover, Richard fears Stanley's fidelity and this section of the scene takes the form of an interrogation. Once again, Richard the arch-dissimulator is himself faced with dissimulation. Stanley, as his opening circumlocution implies (ll. 375–6), is edgy – his repeated use of superlatives ('mighty sovereign', 'mighty liege', 'mighty sovereign', 'Most mighty sovereign') signal a man who is protesting too much. Stanley has seen the summary execution meted out to Hastings and knows that his life may depend on his ability to survive this interview. Despite Richard apparently having the measure of him, Stanley is released to 'go muster men' (l. 412). The sense of relief and slackening of tension is temporary. Richard commands, almost as an afterthought, that Stanley leave his son behind as a hostage.

416 to the end   Four **Messengers** enter in quick succession, the urgency of their movement onto the stage and the burden of their information raising the tempo and the audience's sense of imminent confrontation. At the mention of 'the army of the Duke of Buckingham' Richard's self-possession caves in and he strikes the Third Messenger. Violence is never far from the front of Richard's mind, but this is the first time that the text explicitly demands that he physically assault another. He may, of course, have delivered on his promise to 'strike' and 'spurn' the Gentleman who intervenes at I.ii.36, may even have struck Hastings with the 'blasted sapling withered up' in Act III, scene iv – the director must decide. But, in *Richard III* at least, Richard's violence is generally either executed by proxy or lurks in his language in the form of threats and psychological terrorism. This moment, then, like the amnesiac slips with Catesby and Ratcliffe, serves to illustrate the disintegration of the character. Equally uncharacteristic is the evident sincerity of the consequent apology (in F, Richard gives the messenger a purse of money 'to cure that blow of thine'). Catesby's news of Buckingham's capture (l. 448) offers some cheer, but the fundamental tenor of the end of this scene remains the same: Richmond is at hand. 'The rest march on with me' (l. 455) – a scene which began with Margaret's solitary, quiet induction concludes with the sounds of drums and trumpets and the machinery of war lumbering into gear.

Act IV, scene v

1 to the end A brief scene which compounds our sense of the momentum of events. Stanley meets with **Sir Christopher**, a purely functional character whose job it is to list for us the noblemen who are now rallying to Richmond's cause. Stanley's desertion to Richmond is confirmed, lest we were in any doubt. The greater revelation comes at the scene's conclusion: 'the Queen hath heartily consented / He shall espouse Elizabeth her daughter' (ll. 17–18). The last laugh is hers. Stanley gives Sir Christopher letters for Richmond and the two men part hastily towards opposite exits.

ACT V

Act V, scene i

1 to the end The captured Buckingham is brought on stage, under guard and accompanied by Ratcliffe; we remember the latter's function as a Grim Reaper for Richard's victims from his presence at Pomfret. How much respect has been paid to the prisoner since his capture? As the former second-in-command, the King's 'second self', has he been well treated or conversely humiliated, even tortured? There are the vestiges of a residual respect in Ratcliffe's repetition of 'my lord' (ll. 2, 11), and in the time allowed to the once mighty Duke to meditate on his imminent execution. How much do they fear his escape? Is he manacled as well as guarded, or has he given up the ghost to such an extent that they do not fear physical resistance or escape? Gone is the smooth politician; the suave veneer has peeled away to expose a vulnerable, weary and self-hating figure. The man who bragged of being able to 'counterfeit the deep tragedian' now finds himself deep in his own tragedy. We recognize the convention of the doomed character's retrospecting back to the moment of Margaret's curses (ll. 25–7). All of those present in Act I, scene iii, have now seen her curses fulfilled – all save one. As we see Richard's former ally led off to execution, we cannot help but think that Richard himself is living on borrowed time.

Act V, scene ii

Entry   Drums and trumpets again, but perhaps now with a different rhythm and tone from those of Richard's musicians. This group
of men now entering may also wear differentiated costumes –
perhaps military uniform – to provide a visual as well as aural
contrast to Richard's troops. Leading the congregation of Lords is the
man we can only infer is **Richmond**. Here, at last, is our first sight of
Richard's nemesis. What do we see? If the production wants to read
the play's finale as a straightforward show-down between unequivocal opposites, then the figure of Richmond will embody a Tillyardian
optimism in the benign telos of history. He is the pin-up boy of
regime change. The stage will be bathed in a new light, and the stur-
diest and best-looking young member of the company will combine
righteousness with an earnest sex-appeal to leave us in no doubt that
England will be a better place under his stewardship. Such an interpretation is entirely consonant with the way in which the part is written and the attitudes of other characters toward Richmond.
However, if the director is sceptical of moral absolutes, quick-fix
solutions and politics in general, there is clearly the option to read
against the text's grain, as it were, and present a more pragmatic, less
morally and sexually charismatic man. Perhaps the most iconoclastic
approach to the part – and not one that I am aware of anyone ever
taking – would be to dress him in black and give him a hunched back.
Such an emphasis on what he and Richard have in common would
represent the furthest extreme to which this against-the-grain reading might lead. There is, however, some middle ground between pin-
up and monster. Although we have now heard Richmond's name
many times, we have no idea, of course, what his attitude is to his
own celebrity. Is he a naturally diffident, even weedy character,
pushed by an accident of birth and a bevy of ambitious lords into the
unlikely role of avenging angel and heir apparent? Might we sympathize with someone who has unwillingly had greatness thrust upon
him? This first entrance will do much to establish the nature of our
brief relationship with this pivotal character.

1 to the end   Richmond is flanked by Lords. In Q and F, the
number is indeterminate, although only three speak (F names these

as Oxford, Blunt and Herbert). The preceding scene of Buckingham's death speech has given some members of Richard's army time enough to change. But if the director's human resources are very limited, then it would make good sense to have the actors of Rivers, Grey, Vaughan, Hastings, and even Clarence re-costume and double as Richmond's followers. (They will, of course, be required in Act V, scene iv, as ghosts, but such quick changes are hardly prohibitive.) If lines 17–21 are distributed between the Rivers–Grey–Vaughan actors, there would be an appropriate sense, anticipating the later dream-sequence, that Richard's victims are coming back to haunt him. Once the characterization of Richmond and the casting of his attendant Lords have been decided upon, the tenor of this scene is simple: we are 'but one day's march' (l. 13) away from the climactic battle.

Act V, scene iii

1 to the end   One army replaces the other. Is Richard's decision to stop here capricious? Are his troops expecting merely to cross the stage, as it were? Does the ground that Richard has chosen seem to them propitious or foreboding? (The heavy irony of 'even here in Bosworth field' (l. 1) will not be lost on the audience.) Richard calls for tents to be pitched. Much critical ink has been spilt on the issues of how and when these tents were pitched on the Elizabethan stage, and what we might imagine these tents looked like. Whilst of great interest to historians of original staging practices, the modern director (and reader) has a blank slate on which to re-imagine how these areas should be represented. So far the play's demand for significant props has been light: a chair/throne, a bench, a hearse/stretcher. All of these can be easily carried on and off stage. The demand for tents seems to be of a different order altogether. Memories of disastrous camping holidays spring ineluctably to mind, and one might imagine Richard's soldiers, mallets in hand, scouring the stage for lost pegs. Yet there is no reason why, given stage lighting and the fundamentally symbolic nature of theatrical representation, the 'tents' need be complex objects, literally fabric-ated before our eyes. The 'erection' of the tents could be achieved by casting two discrete blocks of light on either side of the stage, symbolic areas into which synechdochic props can be brought. Just as the presence of a throne evokes the 'whole' palace, so the placing of camp beds and stools will evoke two tents. The audience will willingly piece out the imperfections with their thoughts. To further adapt the Chorus's famous metatheatrical introduction to *Henry V*, 'Think, when we talk of tents, that you see them' (Prologue, l. 26). Whether the Elizabethan spectator saw one, two or no tents at all, we may never know. In our imaginary production, though, the tents can be as literal or as symbolic as the theatre's resources and the production's aesthetic demand.

After the instruction to erect the tents, Richard immediately notices Catesby's expression. His unconvincing response fails to reassure Richard, who calls forth Norfolk for another test of his followers' temperament. It would be tempting to call Richard's behaviour here and elsewhere in the final Act paranoid, if it weren't for the fact that his anxieties of infidelity and desertion are not groundless. He is, oxymoronically, a justified paranoiac. Is there a strained chumminess in that 'ha' (l. 5)? The upbeat bravado Richard displays throughout this short scene momentarily cracks open to reveal a chasm:

> Here will I lie tonight. –
> But where tomorrow? Well, all's one for that. –
>
> (ll. 7–8)

The fear is reflexively suppressed. But Shakespeare is preparing us (and the actor) for a later speech in which Richard will talk to himself – there is even a suggestion in this brief private moment of a splitting of the self:

> New, fearful Richard: 'But where tomorrow?'
> Old, impregnable Richard: 'Well, all's one for that.'

His orders end with a prosaic couplet and a colossal understatement: 'tomorrow is a busy day' (l. 18), immediately contrasted with . . .

Act V, scene iv

1–57 . . . The heightened poetic register of his opponent: 'The weary sun hath made a golden set'. The contrast continues with

Richmond's confident directions and the apparent warmth with which he treats his followers. There is no sign here of the interior neurosis glimpsed in Richard in the preceding scene. If the director and designer have chosen not to construct tent structures, but are establishing the separate camps with furniture props, it will be here that Richmond's 'tent' is set up. Jowett has the direction '*Soldiers bring a table, chairs, ink, and paper into his tent*' after line 20, but there is no reason why the table and chairs shouldn't be set at the beginning of the scene – it would even make more sense of Richmond's demand only for 'ink and paper' (l. 20). As Richmond's party withdraw into the 'tent', Richard's enters on the other side of the stage. A striking 'split-screen' effect is created. This is audaciously non-naturalistic dramaturgy. Richard, too, calls for 'some ink and paper', the verbal parallelism echoing the mirror-imaging of the two camps. (Once again, Richard does not call for a table and chair – have they already been set in the previous scene?) Norfolk and Catesby are despatched, the latter to repeat the threat to Stanley to commit his troops 'lest his son George fall / Into the blind cave of eternal night' (ll. 40–1) – there is some relish in the poetic euphemism. Richard craves reassurance from Ratcliffe as to Lord Northumberland's loyalty (ll. 45–51) and, in asking for some wine, seeks an artificial remedy for his incipient melancholy. Ratcliffe's exit might coincide precisely with the entrance of Stanley to the other camp, thus cross-fading our attention away from the now solitary Richard toward Richmond's more populated stage space. There may, however, be a brief pause for our eye to linger on Richard. If so, it will observe him as we have never seen him before: alone, silent, oblivious for the first time to our presence – a great opportunity, however brief, for the actor to physicalize his mood, to show the world-weariness he has largely had to suppress in front of his followers, and to make voyeurs of us all.

58–96   Minutes ago, Richmond has described the reddish glow of the sunset; now we are deep within a 'dark night' and nudging towards dawn ('flaky darkness breaks within the east', l. 65). Of course, such lines were originally intended to fire the imaginations of open-air, late-afternoon spectators. Now it is up to lighting designers to decide how such indicators should be translated into the play of light, shade and colour on the stage. Stanley promises to relate his news 'In brief' (l. 66) – an ominous indication in Shakespeare that a character is about to speak at some length. He and the Lords leave Richmond alone and the stage composition achieves equipoise with the symmetrical composition of the two generals, the King and the Challenger. It is now Richmond's turn to reveal interiority which he does by offering a prayer, presumably whilst kneeling.

97–155 In Act V, scene i, Buckingham has imagined the 'moody, discontented souls' of all Richard's victims peeping 'through the clouds' and beholding onstage events (ll. 7–8). As Richmond falls asleep, we perhaps have a few seconds to register the surprisingly untheatrical spectacle of two men napping. Such tranquillity is shattered by the irruption of the supernatural and the entrance of the first of a succession of moody souls. The unnerving strangeness of this arrival is compounded by the unfamiliarity of the spectre. Unless we are watching this performance in the context of the tetralogy, we will not know until the mention of Tewkesbury that this is Prince Edward, or until line 106 that the next ghost is that of his father, King Henry VI. The staging of all the ghosts presents an exciting challenge to the director and designer. The most immediate decision concerns their appearance. Is this one of those nightmares – from Richard's perspective at least – in which one's assailants are recognizably as they appeared when alive? Or, like Banquo's Ghost shaking his gory locks at Macbeth, do these spectres' bodies bear the scars of their violent deaths? Do the ghosts retain their original costuming? How, if at all, should their faces be made-up? What will lighting and sound effects contribute to the chill-factor of this passage? Equally important is the question of the ghosts' movement and the extent of their interaction with Richard and Richmond. Are the 'sleeping' men apparently awake for these visitations? Can the ghosts touch, caress, and embrace Richmond and can he respond to these physical benedictions? Can they strike, spit at or even mock-stab Richard? The content of some of the ghosts' speeches seem to suggest corresponding actions and images that might echo and re-create earlier moments. Henry VI speaks of his body being 'punchèd full of deadly holes' (l. 104) – might the ghost here reveal those wounds, incisions which might 'bleed afresh' (I.ii.54) as they did before the wooing of Anne? Clarence's ghost speaks of having been 'washed to death with fulsome wine' (l. 111) – surely the bowl of wine by Richard's side is too tempting a prop not to use here. The Princes' ghosts wish that their memory might 'weigh [Richard] down to ruin' (l. 127) – if Young York has indeed jumped on Richard's shoulders earlier in the play (III.i.131) might this image not be re-created? The addresses to Richmond are naturally less turbulently personal, more formulaic than those to Richard. Most are simply and less dramatically wishing him a good night's sleep. The turmoil on one side of the stage is thus juxtaposed with tranquillity on the other.

As Jowett notes, 'the ghosts enter in the order of their deaths, except that Hastings is brought on between the Princes and Anne, probably because one of the boy actors played both a young prince and Anne' (p. 339n). If, as is likely in the modern theatre, the latter parts are not being doubled, there is no reason why the order of appearance should not be tweaked to match exactly the chronology of the deaths. Furthermore, if none of the ghosts is doubled, the director might choose, instead of the 'one-in, one-out' policy of most editions, to keep all the ghosts on stage after their speeches. This allows for the powerful image of a cumulative mass of victims, an eerie congregation which recapitulates and underlines the sheer number of bodies over which Richard has clambered to the throne. (It is also interesting to note that neither Q nor F provide individual exits for the ghosts.)

156–85   If Richard has with open eyes and active body interacted with the ghosts, he must, for the last part of Buckingham's speech at least, fall back into a sleeping position if only to '*start[eth] up out of a dream*' on Buckingham's exit. (Does Buckingham fade, like the ghost of Hamlet's father, on the crowing of a cock, the same village cock that Ratcliffe informs us has twice saluted the morn, ll. 189–90?) As Richmond sleeps the sleep of the just, we are alone with Richard for the last time in the play. Following Buckingham's injunction, he has been thinking of 'bloody deeds and death' (l. 150) and his body feels as if it has been penetrated ('Bind up my wounds!', l. 156). He is drenched in a cold sweat and his flesh trembles. The lights, the designer might note, 'burn blue' (l. 159). The disjointed, schizophrenic speech is a challenge to the actor. (Harold Bloom: 'I cannot think of another passage, even in the tedious clamor of much of the *Henry VI* plays, in which Shakespeare is so inept', p. 67). How much is shared and aired directly to the audience? Or are we suddenly in a more 'internalized' naturalistic mode, eavesdropping on Richard's self-analysis? Jowett's punctuation of lines 161–71 nicely suggests the bivocal division within Richard; the actor might here tonally differ-entiate each 'voice', much as I implied he might with 'But where tomorrow? Well, all's one for that' (V.iii.8). The second half of the speech is direct and unequivocal. We have never heard Richard speak like this before: 'I shall despair. There is no creature loves me, / And if I die, no soul will pity me' (ll. 179–80). The acknowledgement of his lack of humanity has a paradoxically humanizing effect on our perception of Richard. Shakespeare, but not the character, is clearly here manipulating the audience towards pathos – it is up to the actor to decide how little or how much sympathetic sentiment he wants to generate. Given that Richard cannot even feel pity for himself (l. 181), it may be that there is no appeal to audience pity in this address, rather that it is a clinical, factual self-appraisal.

186 to the end   'My lord'. Are the words disembodied? Do they emanate from the shadows? Richard starts again, fearing more ghosts, only to be reassured by Ratcliffe's self-identification. 'I fear, I fear' (l. 193) – is Richard surprised to hear himself say these words to another? The two men leave in order to eavesdrop, their exit cross-fading into the arrival of lords into Richmond's tent. Richmond has just been described as 'shallow' (l. 198) by Richard, and his response to his dream ('my soul is very jocund', l. 211) has inevitably little of the force or depth of Richard's. It is now 'Upon the stroke of four' (l. 214) – it was 'dead midnight' a few minutes ago (l. 159), and we are on the verge of battle.

Given that only a group of anonymous Lords have entered Richmond's tent, the stage direction/description, '*His oration to his soldiers*', suggests that Richmond steps forward and addresses us. A smattering of onstage soldiers might assemble, but it seems with both this and Richard's oration that the actor should speak directly to the offstage audience in his effort to motivate and inspire. Richmond's oration, supremely confident in its appeal to a suprapersonal power and the justice of his cause, is measured and clearly structured, especially in lines 232–41 with their repeated conditionals. It is also inclusive and proto-democratic ('loving countrymen', l. 216; 'gentlemen', l. 224; 'the least of you shall share his part thereof', l. 247). His drums and trumpets sound 'bold and cheerfully' (l. 248) as he exits purposefully, accompanied by his lords.

Act V, scene v

1 to the end Self-belief is replaced by jittery suspicion: Richard and Ratcliffe enter, perhaps in mid-conversation, or perhaps, in an echo of the opening of Act III, scene vii, from separate directions with Richard once again dependent on a henchman for information. The news is apparently reassuring. The clock that strikes might be an onstage, small portable mechanism (cf. Jowett, p. 336n) – although it is hard to see why Richard would command someone else to 'Tell the clock there' if the object were near him. An offstage church chime might strike an appropriately ominous note here; ask not for whom the bell tolls . . .

Norfolk rushes in to announce that Richmond's army is already in the field. His 'Arm, arm, my lord' (l. 17) implies that Richard should be helped on with his armour during the ensuing bout of instructions (ll. 19–30). The reading of the doggerel couplet that has been planted in Norfolk's tent might produce a moment of vertigo for Richard; he has feared being bought and sold since the crown first touched his head. How convincing for his listeners or himself is the fear-stifling 'A thing devisèd by the enemy' (l. 35)? Having offered an abbreviated motivational speech to those on stage (Ratcliffe, Norfolk and whichever '*others*' the director wants), Richard now turns to us in the audience, as Richmond has before him.

It is only a slight exaggeration to say that, if Richmond's oration resembled a sermon, Richard's takes the tone and tropes of a tabloid editorial. Insistently xenophobic, demotic and alarmist, Richard's energetic and highly colourful language powerfully and entertainingly appeals to our baser instincts. The contents are not logical:

would 'famished beggars, weary of their lives' (l. 58) really have the
energy to 'Ravish our daughters' (l. 66)? But Richard is appealing to
our emotions, not our reason. After the bouts of neurosis, the spectral hallucinations, and the uncharacteristic introspection, it is hard
not to admire the extent to which Richard has pulled his selves
together to make this speech. Like the 'bastard Bretons' (l. 62) we are
'beaten, bobbed, and thumped' (l. 63) by the soaring demagogy of
Richard's speech, and, as the drum sounds off stage and news arrives
of Stanley's desertion, the address reaches its climax. (Incidentally,
does Norfolk know that he is probably saving George Stanley's life by
counselling Richard to execute him after the battle? l. 75.) After the
ghosts, Richard's conscience had 'a thousand several tongues'
(V.iv.172), but now 'A thousand hearts are great within my bosom' (l.
76) – with his speaking part almost over, the actor should here be
sparing nothing to pull out all the vocal stops.

Act V, scene vi

Stage action   *Alarums and excursions*. Drums may well have underscored the end of the preceding scene (from l. 66 onwards), and
before the sound of Richard's words 'Victory sits on our helms' can
fade, trumpets and perhaps more drums fill the auditorium with
the cacophony of warfare. '*Excursions*' can mean whatever the director wants. The main point is to convey a microcosm or snapshot of
battle. Whether the skirmishes that take place mimic 'real' violence
as we imagine it to happen in warfare or whether the mode of
representation draws attention to its own theatricality (slow-
motion, balletic), these excursions cannot but depend on conventions and are, therefore, best kept brief. On the modern stage there
is also the option to enhance (if not replace) the movement of
actors' bodies with sound, lighting and smoke effects. Whilst there
can be a thrill in seeing a well-choreographed and athletically
executed group fight on stage, the theatre really comes into its own
with single combat – despite both orations' insistence on nation-
hood, we are interested in individuals not nations, and these group
skirmishes function to create the contexts in which individuals
meet their fates.

1 to the end As the stage clears of the warring factions, Catesby enters, perhaps meeting Norfolk or perhaps calling for his assistance. He tells us what Shakespeare has decided not to show us, that Richard is enacting 'more wonders than a man / Daring an [and?] opposite to every danger' (ll. 2–3). The loss of his horse is vital, especially if the actor has located Richard's disability/deformity overwhelmingly in his legs. There then follow an entrance and a line which require little comment. (Like the old joke about 'New York, New York', the line is so good he says it twice (ll. 7, 13). Bloodied but unbowed, Richard is obsessed with finding Richmond. The great mind is thinking instinctively, animalistically: Catesby's plea that the quickest way to a horse is to withdraw is treated as if it were a slight on Richard's manhood. 'Slave' (l. 9) may be accompanied by a lashing out. It might streamline the events of the next few seconds if Catesby chooses, or is forced, to exit, leaving Richard alone to be confronted by the entering Richmond. Or, in the non-streamlined version, both Richard and Catesby exit, trumpets sound, soldiers perhaps clash, and only once these have quit the stage do Richard and Richmond enter and meet.

Act V, scene vii

1 to the end In marked contrast to other Shakespearean single combats (Macbeth and Macduff, Hal and Hotspur, Tybalt and Mercutio, Romeo and Tybalt, et al.), the fight between Richard and Richmond is not prefaced by a vocal exchange. Having established the characters' relationship so much by contrast and counterpoint, perhaps Shakespeare was at a loss to know what they could actually say to each other when face to face. We know that Richard must lose. But within the bland direction '*They fight. Richard is slain*' lies a wealth of options for the fight director. At the very least, it seems clear, given Richard's reported intrepidity in the battle so far, that this will not be a push-over or cake-walk for Richmond. The nature of the weapons – which could be anything from spears to bare hands – will help determine how intimate the fight becomes and how easy it is for Richmond to choke or bleed the life out of his opponent. But the audience will feel short-changed if the combat does not, however briefly, afford the possibility of Richard prevailing.

There is some confusion as to what happens to Richard's corpse. Stanley, about to crown Richmond, claims that he has plucked the golden round 'From the dead temples of this bloody wretch' (l. 5). According to the stage direction, Stanley enters *'bearing the crown'*, which can only mean that Richmond drags Richard's body off stage with him, Stanley removes the crown in the wings, then both re-enter. However, a more dramatic option presents itself. If the stage direction *'bearing the crown'* is ignored (and why not?), Richard's body can be left on stage. When Stanley enters he almost immediately removes the crown from Richard. 'Have I plucked off' would then, plausibly, refer to a very recent act indeed; 'This bloody wretch' would be far more diegetic and powerful if Stanley can accompany the line with a gesture to the corpse. If this suggestion is followed, we have the pay-off that after the fight Richard's lifeless body is left alone on stage, a stark and brutal echo of the play's opening and indeed all those other moments in which Richard has exclusively owned both the stage and the rapt attention of his audience.

As a single unit, the play of *Richard III* is now effectively over. But, seen as the concluding part of a tetralogy, it was necessary for Shakespeare now to pan out, as it were, and conclude the play with a recapitulation of the long history of civil war now peacefully resolved by the accession of Richmond and Elizabeth, 'The true succeeders of each royal house' (l. 30). Thus, Richmond's closing speech breaks down into two sections, both culminating with a call for his listeners to shout 'Amen' (ll. 22 and 41). The word 'peace' resounds three times in the closing lines – we are, Richmond is telling us, about to enter into a soporific, inherently undramatic period of history. The corpse of the man who detested the 'weak-piping time of peace' (I.i.24) perhaps lies at or near Richmond's feet and, as the lights fade, we might feel a pang of nostalgia for the bustle and exhilaration of conflict which have occupied our senses since Richard first limped on stage to involve us in his story.

4 Key Productions and Performances

Had Shakespeare established a literary estate to which performance royalties were due after his death, probably more than any of his plays, *Richard III* would have most swelled the coffers in the four centuries since 1616. With a handful of other plays (*Othello*, 1 *Henry IV*, *Macbeth* and *Hamlet*) it has enjoyed a continuous, highly successful stage life from the Restoration to the present day. The title role is a gift that most actors are loath to refuse. The British theatre at least has been dominated for most of its history by actor–managers, towering figures such as David Garrick, John Philip Kemble, William Macready, Charles Kean and Henry Irving, for whom the choice of performing *Richard III* not only confirmed their place within a theatrical tradition, but also often made sound financial sense. In the twentieth century, the rise of the director did little to dent the frequency with which the play was revived, increasingly in conceptual interpretations or in the context of history play cycles, such as the Royal Shakespeare Company's 'This England' double tetralogy of 2000, when *Richard* was seen as the culmination of a historical sequence stretching back to the deposition of Richard II. The range of interpretations and styles of performance has been remarkable. From one Dr Landis who in 1876 hired Tamany Theatre in New York in order to perform Richard alone on stage while all other parts issued from behind opaque screens, to Kathryn Hunter's gender-bending Gloucester in a distinctly inauthentic all-female production at Shakespeare's Globe in London in 2003. From the vast equestrian displays – starring Richard's horse White Surrey – at Astley's amphitheatre in 1856, to the multi-media, avant-garde production of Lin Zhao Hua in Beijing

in 2000, in which, for example, the self-consciously nonchalant staging of Clarence's death in a visually pleasing prison cell was immediately contrasted with unsettling stage-wide projections of gasping
fish heads in pools of blood.

   This chapter will introduce Colley Cibber's adaptation of the play
and four key British performances of *Richard III*, those in which
Edmund Kean (1814), Henry Irving (1877 and 1896), Laurence Olivier
(1944) and Ian McKellen (1990) took the title role. In choosing 'key'
performances, the first three at least are self-selecting: each, in its
own way, stands as a benchmark of interpretation. Richard Eyre's
production starring McKellen has been chosen as a key example of
director's theatre, in which the lead performance must take its place
within a guiding directorial concept. Such a selection is in no sense
intended to be inclusive, exhaustive or representative of the aestheti-
cally and geographically varied stage history of *Richard III*. (For more
detailed and comprehensive accounts, the reader should consult the
titles listed in the Further Reading section.) Here, at least, we can
inspect a handful of landmarks in the eventful landscape of the play's
performance history. The chapter concludes with a brief exploration
of the ways in which *Richard III* has inspired playwrights and directors
to rearrange, adapt and parody Shakespeare's text for the purposes of
dramatic effect, social comment and entertainment.

Colley Cibber's *The Tragical History of Richard III* (1699)

When discussing the stage history of *Richard III* in the eighteenth and
most of the nineteenth centuries, it would be something of a
misnomer to call the play 'Shakespeare's'. The events of *Richard III*
begin at the conclusion of the Wars of the Roses, and Richmond's
accession at the play's close ends an epoch in which 'England hath
long been mad, and scarred herself' (V.viii.23). These sentiments
must surely have resonated with the general public in the 1660s, as
England once again emerged from the divisive and collective
madness of Civil War. Yet when Richard Gloucester first halted onto
the post-Interregnum stage, it was probably to utter the mortal
lines:

The World must now confess, that Monarchs are
Of him, who rules above, the chiefest care.

The year was 1666, the play *The English Princess, or the Death of Richard III* by John Caryll. As the title more than hints, Princess Elizabeth (who never appears in Shakespeare's play) is the unlikely new focus, with Richard and Richmond engaged in a love-rivalry to the death. Shakespeare's *Richard III* may well have been in the repertory of the King's Company in the 1670s and 1680s, but was undoubtedly revived around 1689–90 by the now combined forces of the King's and Duke's companies. The pre-eminent tragedian of the age, Thomas Betterton, having played Richard in Caryll's sententious play, now took the role of Edward IV in Shakespeare. Samuel Sandford, an actor whose stock-in-trade was lurid villainy, took the title role. Colley Cibber was a teenager when this production took place and apparently did not see it; but he knew and admired Sandford's style – 'a harsh and sullen Pride of Speech, a meditating Brow, a stern Aspect, occasionally changing into an almost ludicrous Triumph over all Goodness and Virtue' (Cibber, 1889: I, p. 138) – and this brand of chiaroscuro heavily influenced his adaptation. Cibber's *The Tragical History of Richard III* premiered at the Theatre Royal, Drury Lane, in December 1699. Sandford was contracted to the rival Lincoln's Inn Field company, so it was Cibber himself then who took the lead, impersonating Sandford as he imagined Sandford would have impersonated Richard: in effect, he counterfeited the deep tragedian. The play was not an immediate success and would not be revived until 1704. Only the most clairvoyant cultural analyst could have predicted that Cibber's *Richard* would 'for a couple of centuries [be] probably the most popular play on the English stage' (Wells, 1982, p. 266). Despite sporadic attempts to return to unadulterated Shakespeare during the mid-nineteenth century, it would not be until Henry Irving's 1877 production that Shakespeare's text(s) would become the default option for directors and actors of the play.

What did Cibber do to make Shakespeare's play so extravagantly and enduringly stage-worthy and successful? First, he got rid of the majority of Shakespeare's lines. The adaptation is 40 per cent shorter than the Folio text; furthermore, of Cibber's 2156 lines, only roughly half are verbatim Shakespeare. And nearly a fifth of those are not from *Richard III*, but are transplanted from other Shakespearian history plays. We are left with something like a quarter of the Folio text. (It is mathematically symbolic that the Folio's eleven ghosts shrink from the size of a football team to the number required to make up a hand at bridge.) Richard's share of what remain increases, especially given that Cibber found no room for such characters as Clarence, Hastings, Edward and Margaret (goodbye to most of I.i, and all of I.iii, I.iv, II.i, III.ii, III.iv, III.v and III.vi) and reduces Buckingham's role. As the excision of Margaret implies, Cibber was not interested in the long historical view and obsessive retrospection of Shakespeare's play – the background is filled in quickly in a new first Act which climaxes with Richard's murder of the imprisoned Henry VI, a passage adapted from 3 *Henry VI*, Act V, scene v. (This opening Act was at first censored lest the plight of Henry VI remind the audience of the exiled former king, James II.)

The Restoration theatre was fond of binary struggles between abstract, always capitalized virtues. If Love and Fame did battle in Caryll's earlier treatment (Hankey, pp. 15–17), in Cibber the gloves were off between Ambition and Conscience. To air this bout, Cibber introduces seven new soliloquies for Richard, great opportunities not only for lip-smacking and hand-rubbing relish, but also for the clarification of mental processes and moral abstracts. At the climax of Act III, for example, where Shakespeare at the equivalent point avoids an obvious 'curtain' moment, Cibber leaves Richard on stage alone, after he has accepted the offer of the crown from Buckingham and the Lord Mayor, to speak to the audience:

> Why now my golden dream is out –
> Ambition like an early Friend throws back
> My curtains with an eager Hand, o'rejoy'd
> To tell me what I dreamt is true – A Crown!
> Thou bright reward of ever daring minds,
> O! How thy awful Glory fills my Soul! . . .
> Conscience, lie still – More lives must yet be drain'd,
> Crowns got with Blood must be with Blood maintain'd.
>
> (III.ii.270–5, 81–2)

Cibber also coined some memorable clap-trapping catchphrases: 'Off with his head. So much for Buckingham' (IV.iv.188); 'Conscience avaunt; Richard's himself again' (V.iii.85) – note the identical caesura and cadence – which would match any of Shakespeare's for popularity and theatrical efficacy.

Cibber's own performance as Richard was not universally acclaimed. Aaron Hill declared that Cibber the actor 'was *born* to be *laugh'd* at', and that his Richard consisted of 'the distorted heavings of an unjointed caterpillar' (quoted. in Kalson, pp. 361, 353). The anonymous critic of the *Laureat* wrote that 'when he was kill'd by *Richmond*, one might plainly perceive that the good People were not better pleas'd that so *execrable* a *Tyrant* was destroy'd, than that so *execrable* an *Actor* was silent' (Williamson and Person, p. 362). Yet the success and longevity of Cibber's adaptation was guaranteed by the brilliance which David Garrick brought to the text in the thirty-five years between 1741 and 1776 in which he dominated the English stage. Garrick did more than any actor before or since to enshrine Shakespeare as the national playwright, but his veneration of Shakespeare stopped well short of textual fidelity. Whilst, in the words of his early biographer and friend Thomas Davies, Garrick the actor 'banished ranting, bombast, and grimace; and restored nature, ease, simplicity, and genuine humour' to the stage, Garrick the actor–manager did not choose to banish Cibber and restore Shakespeare's *Richard*. His performances as Richard did much to cement the stage's preference for Cibber over Shakespeare, a preference that would prove remarkably durable: two hundred and fifty years after Cibber's adaptation premiered, not only would Laurence Olivier's film follow Cibber in erasing Margaret from the play, but Richard would also be heard to utter the lines 'Off with his head. So much for Buckingham' and 'Richard's himself again', lines first coined by a young actor–playwright in his late twenties seeking a stage vehicle for his less than persuasive talent for acting tragedy.

Edmund Kean (1814–33)

As the new year of 1814 dawned, Drury Lane Theatre was teetering on the verge of bankruptcy. In the period leading up to 26 January, the company had played 135 nights at a continued loss. On one epoch-making night, the rot stopped. A new tragedian was hired who would transform the theatre's fortunes, and with them the history of English theatre. He premiered as Shylock; as one critic would later remember: 'There came on stage a small man, with an Italian face and fatal eye. . . . His voice was harsh, his style new, his action abrupt and angular' (*Athenaeum*, 18 May 1833). His name was Edmund Kean. Within three weeks he was playing Richard Gloucester in Cibber's adaptation, a performance he would repeat twenty-five times in his first season and which would inject a nightly average of £502 into the ailing box office.

There are two stories to tell about Kean. The first is familiar: this fiery, transgressive, upstart bastard from the provinces arrived in London and with his electrifying presence and vertiginous emotional range revolutionized the English stage. His combination of passion, spontaneity, sublime egoism, dipsomania, and libido; his radical identification with the Other, the outsider and the illegitimate – all these qualities made him an icon of Romanticism. He was a force of nature: jagged as a mountain range, dazzling and nerve-racking as an electrical storm. This is one story; the second complicates without contradicting this dominant narrative. For it is important to remember that Kean was, in some respects, a consummate professional. He is reported to have told David Garrick's widow that: 'Because my style is easy and natural they think I don't study, and talk about the "sudden impulse of genius." There is no such thing as impulsive acting; all is premeditated and studied beforehand' (Cole and Chinoy, pp. 327–8). As 'Betterton', a pseudonymous Philadelphian critic, wrote of Kean in 1821:

> He is called a natural player, but his style of acting is highly artificial and technical; it is uniformly elaborate, systematic, and ambitious. Nothing is left to the inspiration of the moment.   (Cole and Chinoy, p. 330)

The genius of Kean, then, was to make the impulses seem sudden. In this he was clearly not always successful; especially for the multiple-viewer – and who would not want to see Kean more than once? – the overwhelming repetitive consistency of Kean's interpretations must have taken some of the edge off the illusion of spontaneity. But in general his 'systematic' premeditation yielded staggering results.

What did Kean do with Shakespeare–Cibber's text to make his performance as Richard one of the most celebrated in theatre history? Above all, he captured the spirit of the age. As Julie Hankey notes, the notion 'that evil is somehow made more splendid by the aspiring genius of the wrongdoer', and the concomitant attraction to 'the individualism which dared to spurn the common restraints' (pp. 43–4), were key tenets of the Romantic sensibility. That the performance would celebrate individualism was a given. Cibber's text magnifies Richard's role; furthermore, the structure and ethos of the theatre in the early nineteenth century were predicated on competition between individual interpretations. But Kean also embraced the daring aspiration of the role. For William Hazlitt – Kean's most eloquent advocate and sternest critic – he gave 'an animation, vigour, and relief to the part, which we have not seen equalled' (1916, p. 188).

Kean's gift as a performer was the ability to surge energy throughout the auditorium. The efficacy of such bursts depended on contrast, on the alternation between *piano* and *forte*: the 'brief lightning' can only amaze in the context of the 'collied night'. In his notes on public speaking, Kean wrote:

> To crowd every sentence with emphatical words, is like crowding all the papers of a book with Italic Characters, which, as to the effect, is just the same as using no such distinction at all. An emphatical pause is made, after something has been said of peculiar moment, and on which one wants to fix the hearer's attention. Sometimes before such a thing is said, we usher it in with a pause of this nature.
>
> (Quoted in Downer, pp. xvi–xvii)

These moments of emphasis were usually accompanied by a gesture as if to further italicize or 'point' their significance. It is estimated that there were over thirty such 'points' in Kean's performance of Richard. We can reconstruct some of these from contemporary reviews. We also have a unique document, a copy of Kean's promptbook in which the American actor J. H. Hackett annotated 'all of the *business* and *readings* of Mr *Kean* in this play', having watched over a dozen of Kean's performances in New York between 14 November 1825 and 27

November 1826. (Hackett himself performed the entire play in 1826 'in imitation of Mr. Kean'.) From these accounts we can trace the vigorous contrasts between the sardonic and the heroic, between repose and bustle, introspection and extroversion, seduction and violence that formed the performance.

Kean did not appear to aim for a unified, self-consistent reading of the part, but rather played each scene and moment on its own terms. Throughout the first and second Acts, Hackett recurrently describes Kean's delivery with the adverbs 'sneeringly', 'peevishly', 'maliciously' and 'irritably'. As Henry VI expressed his understandable 'misdoubt' of Richard (Cibber, I.iii.18–24), Hackett records that 'Gloster [*sic*] appears hardened against his words and rather inattentive – then shrugs his shoulders at him & chuckles maliciously' (Downer, p. 21). There was ostentatious hypocrisy also in Kean's response to Buckingham's 'Long live Richard, England's royal king!' (III.vii.222). Hackett noted that: 'Richard looses [*sic*] his self command at the word "*King*" from over-joy, squeezes his book [the Bible] to his breast, then instantly checks himself resignedly.' When the stage had cleared he 'bursts out and throws the Book off with violence – walks exultingly' (Downer, p. 60). Such gleeful villainy would be juxtaposed with the moment in the second Act, before the wooing of Anne, when Kean, as if preparing himself for the role of lover, retired away from centre stage and struck a pose downstage right, 'leaning against the side of the stage' to listen to Anne's 23 lines of cursing (Cibber, II.i.66–85). Hazlitt called his attitude 'one of the most graceful and striking ever witnessed on the stage. It would do for Titian to paint.' George Henry Lewes described the moment as 'thoroughly feline – terrible yet beautiful'. The emphasis on the painterly quality of the stage picture reminds us that in a proscenium theatre packed with over 3000 spectators, such tableaux were peculiarly effective in compacting and presenting significance. Kean was often hoarse at the end of an evening trying to project to the rafters of Drury Lane – Leigh Hunt complained that, as the evening progressed, Kean's voice 'resembled a Hackney coachman's at one o'clock in the morning'. But if his voice let him down, he could always speak through his body.

Kean's action was eloquent. Two key examples illustrate how he used his body to express both Richard's humanity and his superhumanity. In the tent scene on the eve of the Battle of Bosworth (V.iv in both Shakespeare and Cibber), Hackett noted that there were 'long pauses in this scene' (Downer, p. 88). One such came after Richard's lines: 'An hour after Midnight, come to my Tent, / And help to Arm me' (Cibber, V.iv.16–17). Here Kean 'stands for some moments fixed in reverie, drawing figures in the sand: this was a boldness which nothing but the consciousness of great talent could venture upon; for no common man dare keep the audience waiting without a speech or a startling attitude' (*The Examiner*, 28 February 1814). The reverie would come to an abrupt end: 'A good night, my friends.' The unexpected moment drew 'shouts of applause' on the opening night. For Leigh Hunt, generally disappointed with the obvious artifice of much of Kean's performance, not least the 'enormous and bolster-like pad' he stuffed into his stocking to suggest deformity, this was a rare and precious moment in which Kean managed to 'unite common life with tragedy – which is the greatest stage desideratum' (quoted in Williamson and Person, p. 379). In April 1814, Byron would remember this dumb-show in his 'Ode to Napoleon' ('Or trace with thine all idle hand, / In loitering mood upon the sand'), just as in *Lara: A Tale* he would evoke Kean's leaning pose before the wooing of Anne, 'With folded arms and long attentive eye'. The piece of business represents creativity of the highest order, finding gaps in between units of text in which to reveal character.

If the sand-drawing mime precisely highlighted Richard's distraction, minutes later in the single combat with Richmond, Kean's body was a whirl of focused demonic energy. Characteristically, the touch of common life gave way to uncommon heroism. Such was Kean's ferocity and daring in these final moments that, for Keats at least, there was always the illusion that the play might have an alternative ending: 'Although so many times he has lost the battle of Bosworth Field, we can easily conceive him really expectant of victory, and a different termination of the piece' (Wells, 1997, p. 52). Hackett's detailed annotation of the stage combat gives us the choreography of these last moments: 'turns upon right side – writhes – rests on his hands – gnashes his teeth at him [Richmond] – as he utters his last

words – blinks – & expires rolling on his back' (Downer, p. 98). But
Hazlitt's description remains definitively evocative:

> He filled every part of the stage. . . . He fought like one drunk with
> wounds: and the attitude in which he stands with his hands stretched out,
> after his sword is taken from him, had a preternatural and terrific
> grandeur, as if his will could not be disarmed, and the very phantoms of
> his despair had a withering power.   (Hazlitt, 1916, pp. 165–6)

Like all truly great actors, Kean inspired in his viewers every shade of
emotion but indifference. Like his near contemporaries Franz Liszt
on the piano and Niccolò Paginini on violin, Kean was part of a wider
culture of performance in which dazzling virtuosity, technique and a
whiff of vulgar showmanship combined to intoxicate audiences
throughout Europe in the first decades of the nineteenth century.
Kean remains a byword for the affective power of the actor. The
sword with which he fought when drunk with wounds was destined
to become a totemic heirloom, passed from actor to actor as if to arm
them with the 'preternatural and terrific grandeur' of Kean's Richard.

Henry Irving (1877 and 1896)

Reading the opinions of Henry Irving's detractors always reminds me
of the notorious MGM screen-test verdict handed out to Fred Astaire
at the beginning of his career: 'Can't act. Can't sing. Balding. Can
dance a little'. Henry James wrote of Irving that 'His personal gifts –
face, figure, voice, enunciation – are rather meager' and that his
acting was that 'of a very superior amateur' (1949, pp. 36–7); watching
Irving's first Richard in 1877 he averred: 'Of what the French call
diction – of the art of delivery – he has apparently not a suspicion' (p.
103). As William Archer noted, 'There has probably never been an
actor of equal prominence whose talent, nay whose mere compe-
tence has been so much contested' (quoted in Donaldson, 1970, p.
46). 'For an actor who can't walk, can't talk and has no face to speak
of, I've done pretty well,' Irving once admitted to Ellen Terry (Craig,
p. 69). But it was to this young actor that Kean's sword was presented

after his first London performance of Richard III, a presentation that recognized the innovative and authoritative nature of Irving's approach to text, scenery and character interpretation. The categories are artificial – each component of course interacts with the others – but it is convenient to examine each in turn.

Text

Irving was not the first actor–producer to attempt to overturn decades of convention by staging Shakespeare rather than Cibber's text. His way was fitfully paved by William Macready, who, for two performances in 1821, reintroduced Margaret and Clarence, whilst retaining most of Cibber's interpolations. In 1845 and 1849 Samuel Phelps went further in discarding Cibber altogether – his eventual decision in 1861 to return to Cibber was curious given the enthusiasm of critics for the revelatory new balance that the presence of Margaret especially brought to the play. In Manchester in 1870, Charles Calvert again resurrected undiluted – though as always, cut and spliced – Shakespeare. But it was the cumulative success of Irving's two productions in 1877 and 1896 that, combined with a wider trend towards authenticity, academicism, and textual integrity, led to a point of no return in the stage history of the play: stamped with the authority of Irving's prestige and (at least in 1877) the approval of the paying public, Shakespeare's text was here to stay.

Irving cut 1600 lines from Shakespeare, just over 40 per cent, but perhaps owing to elaborate scene changes and the protraction of Irving's vowels, the 1896 performance lasted for two hours and forty minutes. The play was divided into fifteen scenes; the whole of Act I took place on 'A Street'. Act V alternated twice between Richmond's and Richard's 'encampments' before the fifth scene's climax at Bosworth Field: the illusion of reality so carefully constructed thus far would have been shattered by the collocation of the rival tents, so Irving had to switch between them in separate scenes. Given that a curtain would fall at the end of each Act, Irving strove to bring it down with a bang. Act II ended with 'Chop off his head, man. Something we will determine' (III.ii.190); Act III with Buckingham's resounding 'Long live Richard, England's royal king' (IV.i.222), and the production's closing line became 'A horse! A horse! My kingdom for a horse!' followed by combat and crowning, thus eliminating the 47 lines which follow in Shakespeare. As this final cut implies, despite the greater potential in Shakespeare's text for a balance between Richard and the supporting characters, Irving effectively followed Cibber in the Richard-centric emphases of his cutting and streamlining. While the return to Shakespeare might have led to a revaluation of the play's economy of attention and personality, the effect of the heavy cutting was to rob most other characters of any substance. A. B. Walkley complained:

> The stage is bathed in blood and piled in corpses. But, as a matter of fact, we feel neither pity nor terror. For who are these hapless victims . . . ? They enter, speak a few words, and are gone. Virtually they have no character, no existence, nothing we can grow accustomed to.　(Quoted in Colley, pp. 140–1)

Although she is not one of Richard's 'hapless victims', this well describes Margaret's participation in Irving's first revival, in which Kate Bateman appeared only in Act I, scene iii. In 1896, however, Irving brought Genevieve Ward's formidable Margaret back on for the all-female lamentation in Act IV, scene iv. If the restoration of Shakespeare's text did not generally serve to throw a new light on hitherto underexposed characters, it at least led one critic to announce that 'Genevieve Ward's Queen Margaret was the outstanding feature of the performance' (Odell, 1963: II, p. 388), a remarkable testimony to the rediscovered dramatic potential of the role.

Although content to cut whole swathes of the play, Irving nevertheless clearly thought long and hard about the interpretive implications of keeping or cutting even the smallest of passages; especially, one might add, if those passages were Richard's. In the collection of artefacts relating to Irving's career assembled by his manager Bram Stoker (better known as the author of *Dracula*), there are two varying prompt copies of the 1896 *Richard III*. The first seems to represent the text as it was prepared for rehearsals; the second, annotated by Irving himself, appears to reflect changes made at some point before or during the run. Intriguingly, this section of Richard's opening soliloquy was originally cut:

And therefore, since I cannot prove a lover
To entertain these fair well-spoken days,
I am determinèd to prove a villain,
And hate the idle pleasures of these days.

(I.i.28–31)

These lines are, however, handwritten in at the bottom of the page in the first prompt copy, which was presumably sent back to the printers who then reinstated the lines in the second. But Irving changed his mind again. In the second copy, he draws a neat line through them. We can only assume that he settled on saying:

Unless to spy my shadow in the sun
And descant on mine own deformity.
Plots have I laid . . .

(I.i.26–7, 32)

Did he speak the excised lines in rehearsal, even on the opening night, and find them somehow inappropriate? Was the link between not being a lover and being a villain too psychologically shallow for Irving? Was the emphasis on hatred too charged for the subtle, mocking Richard he wanted to show at the play's opening? T. S. Eliot wrote in 'Prufrock' of how 'In a minute there is time / For decisions and revisions which a minute will reverse' – Irving's second and third thoughts serve as a paradigm for the shifting, provisional quality of live theatre.

Scenery

A. B. Walkley claimed that it was not as an actor but as a scenographer, or *metteur-en-scène*, that Irving had performed the greatest service to Shakespeare:

His series of Shakespearean land and seascapes, Veronese gardens open to the moonlight, a Venice unpolluted by Cook's touristry, groves of cedar and cypress in Messina, Illyrian shores, Scotch hillsides, and grim castles, Bosworth Field – what a panorama he has given us! The sensuous, plastic, pictorial side of Shakespeare had never been seen before he

showed it. Here you have the flamboyant artist outdoing Delacroix on his
own ground.   (Walkley, p. 260)

When Irving first starred in *Richard*, he was not yet both actor and
manager of the Lyceum. As Alan Hughes notes, the first production
was mounted 'on a very modest scale' with only ten fairly rudimentary sets (p. 156). In 1896, however, Irving deployed the fullest range
of plastic and panoramic resources available, to create a striking variety of locations. Irving was the pioneer (in England, at least) of the
now conventional practice of lowering the house lights during
performances. From this semi-darkness, his audience gazed at the
glowing, proscenium-framed playing space as at an enormous
canvas on which Irving's expert sense of colour, harmony, composition, tonal contrasts and architectural detail created a succession of
captivating images. The gaze would be disrupted as the curtain
lowered to allow an army of stage hands to change sets between
scenes, but the ensuing revelation as the curtain rose again made the
often lengthy waits worthwhile. According to Madeleine Bingham,

> The whole production was in the best realistic style, from the picturesque
> streets of old London and the gloom of the Tower to the scene in the
> Council Chamber (most substantially constructed with broad, massive
> stairs and a lofty gallery). In the battle scene a tent occupied the whole
> stage, complete with a luxurious couch, armour lying about, a coal fire
> burning in a brazier, and with a flap of the tent pulled aside to afford a
> view of the battlefield.   (p. 116)

Representative of his stagecraft were the visual and aural settings and
the choreography of bodies in space that preceded the wooing of
Anne. In this, Irving had tried to make three-dimensional a recent
painting by the Royal Academician Edwin A. Abbey which depicted
Richard waylaying Anne in front of a sea of hooded mourners
including, improbably, two small Prince-like figures. Seymour Hicks
remembered 'the weird lighting; the tolling of the bell; the shadowy
procession bearing the dead king to his tomb' (Saintsbury and
Palmer, p. 117). Bram Stoker recalled how 'the tide of mourners seems
to sweep along in resistless mass, with an extraordinary effect of the
spear-poles of royal scarlet amidst the black draperies' (Stoker: I,

p. 126). Archer found the richness of the designs, the uniformly 'highly-coloured, fashion-plate' costumes and the conscious striving for Beauty somewhat cloying: 'Richard himself, while he talks of "entertaining tailors to adorn his body", has already the price of half a county on his back' (Williamson and Person, p. 401).

Interpretation

When we talk about 'Irving's Richard' we are talking about two very different productions, separated by almost as many decades. The younger Richard was more obviously embittered at the hand that Nature had dealt him. Yet in 1877 the major keynote of Irving's later interpretation was firmly sounded. As Dutton Cook noted:

> Throughout the play, indeed, the desire of the actor appears to be to depict *Richard* not as the petulant, vapouring, capering, detonating creature he has so long been represented in the theatre, but as the arch and polished dissembler, the grimmest of jesters, the most subtle and the most merciless of assassins and conspirators.   (Cook, pp. 328–9)

Such a decoding of intention must have gratified Irving. In a magazine article of 1893 he described how Richard was one of his favourite parts by setting his own interpretation in context. Previous actors, he wrote, had been 'monuments of crime – lowering, truculent, robustious, extremely effective in the blood and bombast vein'. But Shakespeare's Richard – and Irving's acting style – demanded something closer to the ideal against which Hazlitt had judged Kean; Irving wrote:

> Shakespeare's Richard is a Plantagenet with the imperious pride of his race, a subtle intellect, a mocking, not a trumpeting duplicity, a superb daring which needs no roar and stamp, no cheap and noisy exultation. . . . In this character, as in Iago, the great element is an intrepid calculation. (Irving, p. 239)

William Archer noted that Irving spoke the lines about high birth and the cedar's top 'with memorable greatness' (Williamson and Person, p. 400). 'I often wonder', said Tennyson when Irving first

played the part, 'where Irving gets his distinctive *Plantagenet* look'
(Saintsbury and Palmer, pp. 116–17). Many traditional points beloved
of the old actors were under-played or eliminated. The rebuke of
Buckingham and the words 'Thou troublest me. I am not in the vein'
(IV.ii.120) were, according to Joseph Knight, 'spoken with the species
of irony which is common with Richard, and not with the angry snarl
that usually accompanies them' (Williamson and Person, p. 399).
Shaw complained in 1896 that after the coronation scene Irving
laboured too hard after the pathetic and the sublime; the critic
preferred the 'craftily mischievous, the sardonically impudent'
Punch-like impersonation of the first three Acts (Shaw, 1961, p. 164;
see also Chapter Six: Critical Assessments). Henry James, although
ambivalent towards Irving, wrote that in the 1896 production he did
'what he does best': 'makes, for the setting, a big, brave general
picture, and then, for the figure, plays on the chord of the sinister-
sardonic, flowered over as vividly as may be with the elegant-
grotesque' (James, p. 287). The sinister-sardonic Irving was nicely
represented by the moment when Richard knelt to his mother to
crave her blessing:

> Irving, with a refinement of mockery, lightly spreads his handkerchief on
> the ground at her feet before kneeling to her. This little touch is thrown in
> with such finish that it is not till he rises again with the ironical *aside* that
> follows ['And make me die a good old man . . .' (II.ii.96ff.)] that its ribald
> insolence is made clear'.   (Quoted in Colley, p. 137)

Although in the opening soliloquy and in the silent minutes in his
tent, Irving offered the naturalistic spectacle of a character unaware
of his audience, in the business with the handkerchief, the scene with
the Lord Mayor at Baynard's Castle, and the wooing of Anne, he,
conversely, stepped out of the fictional frame to nudge and wink at
the audience. Of the exchange with Anne ('Ill rest betide the chamber
where thou liest. / So will it, madam, till I lie with you. / I hope so. / I
know so', I.ii.110–12), Archer wrote that the last three words were
spoken 'with a humorous leer at the audience, never attempting to
make them carry, as it were, and impress Lady Anne. If she hears
them at all (he treats them almost as an aside) she cannot fail to
realise that he is laughing in his sleeve at her' (Williamson and Person,

p. 400). Shaw regretted that Irving played the scene 'as if he were a Houndsditch salesman cheating a factory girl over a pair of second-hand stockings' (1961, p. 170). In their dealings with the Lord Mayor and the burghers, Richard and Buckingham were 'scarcely at pains to hide the tongue in the cheek' (*Athenaeum*, 26 December 1896). The moment-to-moment variety of an interpretation that shifted, or was perceived to shift, between lofty Plantagenet and seedy salesman, between high naturalism and tongue-in-cheek anti-illusionism, reminds us that live performance is often a contradictory affair that resists unequivocal description.

There is a caricature of Irving as Richard by Alfred Bryan ('AB') in the Bram Stoker Collection (see Hughes, p. 153, for a companion drawing by the same artist). Irving stands in profile, one matchstick leg crooked, tapering down to long, winkle-picker slippers; the page-boy black hair rests on fur-lined shoulders and a beak-like Robin Hood hat perches on his head. At his feet, no taller than knee-high to this grasshopper, whirl a bevy of little Richards. Ermined scrappers, they swing swords, saw the air and tragically hyperventilate – one looks distinctly like Kean belligerently under alcoholic influence. The key to the whole caricature seems to me to rest on the bridge of Irving's nose: a pince-nez. Here is the student-scholar, the enlightened dignitary high above the 'truculent, robustious' Lilliputian Richards of yesteryear. It would not have been inappropriate (if a little didactic) for Irving to have nestled Shakespeare's text to his breast.

Laurence Olivier (1944)

In such canonical roles as Richard, the anxiety of influence runs high for actors. Irving's performances in the late nineteenth century had effectively consolidated a paradigm of interpretation. Reviewing John Laurie in the role at Stratford in 1939, the *Times* critic averred that 'Richard gives the modern actor the choice of making him a psychological case or a striking piece of theatricality' (quoted in Colley, p. 167). That such a simple contrast between introspection

and extroversion could be made at all owed much to the posthu-
mous influence of Irving's interpretation. When Laurence Olivier
prepared to play the role in 1944, he was haunted by the memory of
two actors who broadly embodied the psychological and theatrical
approaches to the part. From 1942 onwards, the great barn-storming,
blood-and-thunderer Donald Wolfit offered a Richard devoid of
introspection: his performance 'from the mounting of the throne to
the death on Bosworth Field' was, James Agate declared, 'the finest bit
of Shakespearian acting of the robustious order I can remember in
twenty-five years' (1946, p. 36). In an interview with Kenneth Tynan
in the mid-1960s, Olivier remembered his anxiety in playing the part
so soon after this strong and successful interpretation: 'I had seen
[Wolfit's performance], and when I was learning it I could hear nothing but Donald's voice in my mind's ear, and see nothing but him in
my mind's eye. And so I thought, "This won't do, I've just got to think
of something else" ' (Burton, p. 23). The desire 'not to look the same
as another actor' paradoxically led Olivier to remember a less immediate rival: 'First of all I heard imitations of old actors imitating Henry
Irving; and so I did, right away, an imitation of these old actors
imitating Henry Irving's voice – that's why I took a rather thin kind of
vocal address' (p. 23). ('Old men forget', sometimes creatively: twenty
years later in 1986, Olivier said he could not trace the origin of his
Richard voice, claiming he might have heard it 'maybe on a bus or
train, in a church or from a politician's mouth – who knows?' Olivier,
1986, p. 120.)

Unlike Garrick, Kean and Irving, Olivier had been on the London
stage for twenty years before playing Richard. The role had evidently
lost some of its cachet. The *Times* review of Olivier began by acknowledging that 'Some years ago audiences appeared to find the utter
villainy of Richard Crookback something of a stumbling block.'
Attracted to ambiguity and contradiction, these 'children of an
intensely analytical period' were more interested in plays which deli-
cately probed the human condition; so much so, that *Richard III* was
'in danger of losing its place among the histories which are frequently
played' (*The Times*, 14 September 1944). But, as both Wolfit and Olivier
recognized, the fascinated fear and loathing exerted on the British
public by Hitler brought a new dimension to the reception of the

play. For the *Times* reviewer, in September 1944, it was 'painfully evident that the wickedness which defies analysis is not a mere figment of Shakespeare's imagination'. This was by no means a weak-piping time of peace: those who took their seats in the New Theatre read the following announcement in the programme: 'You will be notified from the Stage if an Air Raid Warning has been sounded during the performance – but that does not mean that an air raid will necessarily take place.' Each audience member had the option to leave while the performance continued, with the programme politely requesting: 'All we ask is that – if you feel you must go – you will depart quietly and without excitement' (Theatre Museum Collection).

If the historical timing was propitious for eliciting a heightened audience-response, there was also, of course, the deep advantage of Olivier's distinctive, even paradoxical approach to character, and the physical and mental reserves he brought to every role he played. On the one hand, Olivier began by assembling 'extraneous externals' – the thin voice, the over-sized nose – working from 'the outside in', as he put it (Burton, p. 23). On the other, Olivier had recently been given what he often referred to as the best advice of his career by Tyrone Guthrie: 'if you can't love [a character], you'll never be any good in him' (Burton, p. 21). So, from the inside out, Olivier learned to see Richard from his own point of view: 'When I came to it, I loved Richard and he loved me, until we became one' (Olivier, 1986, p. 122). 'Richard loves Richard' (V.iv.162) – but Richard also loved Larry. Olivier saw self-love and narcissism as vital to the actor's art; it might be argued that he combined these with his fear of rivals, the need to disown antecedents and the paranoia he felt in the lead-up to opening night to produce a brilliant identification between actor and character. Although often cited as the antithesis of the Method actor, Olivier clearly drew on his own fears and desires as an actor to understand Richard. The result for J. C. Trewin, as for many other critics, was a 'marriage of intellect and dramatic force, of bravura and cold reason' which distinguished Olivier's Richard from any other in living memory. He was described as a 'limping panther'; there were scenes in which 'the eloquent eyes, the sharply pointed nose, thin lips and dark wig [had] an almost Cavalier grace' (*The Times*). Some fine romantic flourishes were retained, as if to acknowledge the pantomimic power of illustrious predecessors such as Garrick and Kean. The rejection of Buckingham, for example, was physically virtuosic:

> From the window in Baynard's castle where he stands, Richard leaps down, tossing his prayer book over his shoulder, to embrace Buckingham and exult over their triumph. In mid-career he stops, mindful of his new majesty; and instead of a joyful hug, Buckingham sees the iron-clad hand of his friend extended to him to be kissed, and behind it, erect in horrid disdain, the top-heavy figure of the King of England. (Tynan, p. 35)

The moment was too good for Olivier not to import it into his film. If the subjugation of Buckingham chillingly revealed Richard's monstrous monomania, other pieces of business invited the audience to warm to Olivier's sardonic vision of the role. When handed Hastings's head in a bag, 'he peeps in with wistful intentness, looking almost elegiac – then, after a pause, hurriedly turns the bag as he realizes he has been looking at the head upside down' (Tynan, p. 34). One of the oldest tricks in the vaudevillian book was thus given a villainous twist.

James Agate recognized that 'There was a great deal of Irving in Wednesday's performance, in the bite and devilry of it, the sardonic impudence, the superb emphases, the sheer malignity and horror of it' (1946, p. 110). But there were also strong contrasts. A more sexually charismatic, if not threatening actor than his illustrious predecessor, Olivier played the wooing of Anne without the knowing nudges and winks of Irving's 'Houndsditch salesman':

> I decided to liberate in every pore of my skin the utmost libertinism I could imagine. When I looked at her, she couldn't look at me; she had to look away. And when she looked away, I would spend my time devouring the region between her waist and upper thigh. Shocking, maybe, but right, I felt.   (Olivier, 1986, pp. 117–18)

In the soliloquies Olivier also broke with tradition and directly addressed the audience. It was said of Irving that his opening soliloquy

'resembles what the poet probably intended – the unconscious medi-
tative utterances of a man thinking aloud while wrapt in a fit of
profound abstraction' (Pascoe, quoted in Colley, p. 133). Olivier, by
contrast, immediately took the audience into his confidence. 'We are
positively tipped the wink,' wrote Agate: ' "Grim-visaged war hath
smooth'd his wrinkled front, I don't think"; Mr Olivier may not say
those last three words; his eyebrows certainly signal them' (1946, p.
110). Despite nerves and a gnawing sense that the production would
prove a failure, Olivier's first entrance on opening night stamped his
authority on the role. W. A. Darlington wrote:

> As he made his way downstage, very slowly and with odd interruptions
> in his progress, he seemed malignity incarnate. All the complications of
> Richard's character – its cruelty, its ambition, its sardonic humour –
> seemed explicit in his expression and his walk, so that when he at last
> reached the front of the stage and began the speech, all that he had to say
> of his evil purpose seemed to us in the audience less like a revelation than
> a confirmation of something we had already been told. (Quoted in
> Colley, p. 174)

By the next day's matinee, Olivier was so giddy with success, so
certain of his Richard being loved that as he approached the audience
for the first time 'I actually forgot to limp for a step or two before calling myself to order' (Olivier, 1986, p. 112).

If Olivier's performance inevitably dominates accounts of the
production, reviewers also spared a few column inches for the design
and surrounding cast. Morris Kestleman's set 'had the expressionistic
quality of a mediaeval painting: a tumble of picturesque toy buildings
in streets diminishing in perspective' (Williamson, p. 175). Williamson
also noted the original directorial touches of having Jane Shore
moving 'seductively across the first scene, a laughing and sensuous
ghost from whose embrace Lord Hastings tore himself at his first
appearance', and the 'more effective interpolation' of 'Anne, a wan and
sleepless spectre, sitting immobile at the side of the stage throughout
the coronation scene' (p. 175). The director John Burrell was also
praised for his unobtrusive stage groupings, for the well-judged, tense
silences during the impeachment of Hastings, and for creating the illusion of the ghosts materializing and fading like shadows – 'for once,'

wrote Trewin, 'we cannot mistake the line for a dispirited queue'. As in Irving's 1877 production, Margaret appeared in Act I, scene iii, but not in Act IV, scene iv: in her only appearance, Dame Sybil Thorndike 'pour[ed] the acid so generously that we are sorry to miss a second draught' (Williamson and Person, p. 419).

Ralph Richardson, fresh from a personal triumph in *Peer Gynt* in the same Old Vic season and instantly recognizable to 'the new and film-conscious West End audience', played Buckingham 'with a kind of humane splendour, representing both English majesty and solid yeoman English worth'; the production's historical context perhaps ensured that Richmond's last speech was deeply felt as 'the triumphant clarion of peace' (Williamson, p. 176). Although Richardson would later play Buckingham in Olivier's screen version, relations between the actors were apparently strained by a competitiveness that had underscored the entire season. When the company toured Europe, Olivier insisted that *Richard III* – *his* show – open the tour in Paris. It did, to great acclaim; according to Olivier, Richardson burst into his hotel room late that evening in a jealous rage and made as if to throw his rival off the balcony: 'For a brief moment, he'd wanted to kill me' (1986, p. 206). The duel between Richard and Richmond had spilled off stage. 'If he'd dropped me,' Olivier wryly commented, 'I'd have been acting with Henry Irving much sooner than I'd appreciated' (p. 207). When originally offered the role, Olivier had worried that 'I was being asked to do Richard III to put me in my place' (p. 116) – the performance *did* indeed put him in his place as the most exhilarating British actor of the twentieth century, figuratively if not, by a whisker, literally alongside Irving as the most notable Richard of his generation.

Ian McKellen and Richard Eyre (1990–2)

The three case studies of production offered so far have largely focused on the central interpretation of the eponymous character, a focus which reflects the actor-managerial, aristocratic and Richard-centric ethos of Cibber's adaptation and therefore most of the play's performance history. More than any other play in the canon, *Richard*

III seems to render the director redundant. Is there not already a director on stage, guiding our attention from the privileged downstage
platea position, dominating proceedings and offering a one-man,
ready-made interpretation all other actors/characters are powerless to
contradict? Every production of *Richard III* is destined to be remembered for its lead performance: that is part of the inbuilt mnemonics
of the play. Even so, the onstage dictator can work in tandem with the
offstage director, as several key productions of the mid- to late twentieth century proved. Richard Eyre's production of the play at the
Royal National Theatre in 1990 provides an example of 'director's
theatre' that will form the final case study in this survey of key revivals.

Like all major productions of frequently revived plays, this one
had to distinguish itself from and compete with the memory of
recent revivals. As with any commercial product, novelty and innovation are central to success. The most lauded *Richard* of the 1980s
was that directed by Bill Alexander for the Royal Shakespeare
Company in 1984 with Antony Sher in the title role. This production
has generated an enormous amount of commentary (see Further
Reading), but its defining characteristics, at the risk of being reduc-
tive, can be summarized as: (1) an impressive Gothic medieval
aesthetic that eschewed obvious contemporary relevance in favour
of a richly textured world of tombs, rosaries and pageant; (2) a very
full text and due weight given to supporting characters and thus the
theme of retribution; (3) at the centre, Sher's gymnastic, unapologet-
ically bravura Richard, a spider on crutches, dark, explosive and
sardonic. It could be said that Eyre and McKellen's approach to the
play, whether consciously or not, defined itself in contrast to the
aesthetic and lead performance of Alexander's production. Both a
medieval setting and a virtuosic display of disability must have been
ruled out at a very early stage in the production's planning. In Sher's
Year of the King, the actor recalls the moment when designer Bill
Dudley unveiled the model for the cathedral-like set; director Bill
Alexander commented to his cast: 'As you can see, we resisted the
worst idea we came up with – setting the play in Orwell's 1984 with
high grey walls and giant portraits of Tony Sher everywhere' (Sher, p.
169). Something like this 'worst idea' would be profoundly productive six years later for Eyre and McKellen.

It is relatively common for directors to find parallels between the events of *Julius Caesar* or *Coriolanus* and the rise of fascism in Europe in the 1930s. Although *Caesar* at least has its share of the supernatural, both plays are clearly 'about' political systems and the material struggles between individuals and factions that determine the distribution of power. Although Olivier and Wolfit drew parallels between Shakespeare's and Germany's tyrants during the Second World War, directors have generally fought shy of making full-blown comparisons, perhaps fearing that the centrality of curses, ghosts, and providence to *Richard III* would undercut a political reading. For Eyre, however, 'The rise of a dictator and the political thuggery that goes with it are the main topics of the play. We did not have to look far for analogies, the twentieth century has sophisticated tyranny beyond the dreams of the previous two millennia' (Eyre, p. 134). Where Eyre sought and found his analogy was in mid-1930s Britain, specifically both in the unsavoury rise to prominence of Sir Oswald Mosley and in the Nazi-sympathetic elements within the upper echelons of the Establishment, not least in the royal family itself. In Philip Roth's novel *The Plot Against America* (2004), we are asked to imagine an alternative American history, one in which the national aviator hero and pro-Nazi Charles Lindbergh defeats Franklin D. Roosevelt in the presidential election of 1940. Eyre's concept traded on a similarly unsettling 'it-might-have-happened-here' hypothesis.

In contrast to Bill Alexander's production, this was a starkly secular reading. For example, cruentation, the early modern popular belief that a murdered corpse would spontaneously bleed anew if approached by the murderer, was scrapped from the Lady Anne scene as unbefitting a rational age. The cod-medieval depiction of the nave of Worcester Cathedral was replaced by Bob Crowley's 'empty model box . . . a world of prisons and cabinet rooms and hospital corridors, palaces and areas of ceremonial display set off against candle-lit areas of private pain' (Eyre, p. 135), all evoked with stylish economy. Crowley's black-box set presented, as Martin Hoyle wrote, 'an emptiness, like an empty soul, ready to be filled by the first opportunist' (*Financial Times*, 27 July 1990). In the promptbook, scenes were given titles such as 'Victoria Station' and 'Early morning Downing St.' Such locales were simply and strikingly established. At the end of the second Act, a small, internally illuminated toy train (with which Young York had just been playing) sped across the darkened stage, a night train carrying the future king to his capital. (And, incidentally, a punning reference to Buckingham's advice that the Prince travel to London with 'some little train', II.ii.107.) A red carpet was unrolled across the length of the forestage, station sound effects of train whistles merged with billows of steam, royal parade guards flanked the stage-right wall ready for inspection, and we were expertly placed within one of the great London stations. Downing Street, the residence of the Prime Minister, Lord Hastings, and the general atmosphere of Westminster were conveyed through personal props such as dossiers, telegrams and leather briefcases.

The topography of the production was faithful to the dominant metrocentrism of Shakespeare's text. For most of the production we were trapped in an increasingly sinister, summarily brutal city-scape, one which recalled 'both Alfred Hitchcock movies and Graham Greene novels from the eve of World War II' (Rich, p. 754). It was all the more striking, then, when a backdrop depicting 'Sunlit Uplands' (promptbook) flew in for Richmond's first entrance (V.ii). The image of gently undulating hills, nestling cottages and, focusing the eye, a small village church steeple, offered a sentimentalized pastiche of Constable's Dedham Vale and a moving, if highly manipulative, icon of Englishness. Some critics saw irony or even cynicism in this rosy pastoral: Lois Potter perceptively suggested that 'the green landscape may simply be Richmond's own propaganda poster' (*Times Literary Supplement*, 3–9 August 1990). But this was not, for what it's worth, the director's intention. Eyre wrote:

> Richmond's entrance is set against a backdrop of a peaceful country village with a church. If I was asked what I was defending, it would be this idealized picture of England, which to me is much more than a metaphor, not an intellectual conceit but literally a heart's land.   (Eyre, p. 139)

As if to clinch Richmond's association with a quintessential spirit of England, when he woke in Act V, scene iv, one of his Lords brought him the national panacea, a steaming mug of tea. In the programme, McKellen wrote: 'Our production is not an adaptation, nor even an interpretation. We hope, above all, to present the story clearly, so that you are free to have your own individual response.' Methinks the actor doth protest too much. All reproduction is interpretation, and this production more than most sought, through a conceptual rendering of the play, to guide individual response with a strong arm. Elsewhere in the programme, under the heading 'Tyranny', were quotes from an array of twentieth-century *bêtes noires*: Stalin, Hitler, Goering, and, in bold type-face – perhaps because he was the most plausible locus of the production's interpretation – the home-grown would-be tyrant, Sir Oswald Mosley: 'The only method we shall employ will be the English ones. The good old English fist.' Whilst McKellen's programme note attempted in a way typical of the rhetoric of much Anglophone Shakespearian production to disavow 'interpretation' and privilege the freedom of response of the individual spectator, there were nevertheless many moments in which the interpretive thrust of the production was about as subtle as Mosley's 'good old English fist'. The *coup de théâtre* that formed the climax of the first half was an obvious example. Richard appeared up stage on an elevated hydraulic platform, flanked by his bogus priests. At floor level, his black-shirted followers bore mock-medieval torches, and aggressively oversaw the manipulation of the Mayor of London. On Buckingham's 'Long live Richard, England's worthy King!' the theatre began to reverberate to an amplified series of 'Amen's which, as they crescendoed, morphed into the unmistakable cadence of a Nuremburgian 'Sieg heil!' Richard was now alone, and the platform on which he stood thrust downstage and further upwards, and, while those in the front stalls craned their necks, McKellen's right arm inexorably rose into a hideous salute, which, save for the clenched rather than outstretched palm, was pure Nazi.

These broad, melodramatic flourishes were complemented, if not supported, by an impressive range of small-scale directorial details. The sense of court and political rituals – rituals of dining, staged photographs, cabinet meetings – and Richard's characteristic control and disruption of them was richly conveyed. In Act II, scene i, Richard entered the scene of false reconciliation sporting a black arm band, a sign of mourning for Clarence which went unnoticed by others at first and which proleptically suggested the pseudo-Nazi bands which would later be sported by his ministers and military. As Elizabeth declared the day to be kept holy hereafter, and urged Edward to make amends with Clarence (ll. 71–4), the court arranged itself to face out for a formal photograph. After a prolonged flash – during which the audience laughed at the wit of the conceit – Richard broke both the picture and our laughter with 'Why, madam, have I offered love for this', and the superficial cohesion of the court was returned to chaos. The first court scene (I.iii) was a candle-lit dinner party in which the Queen and her sons (frivolous rich-boys who would have been at home in the Drones Club) were forced to share the same charged social space as their long-standing enemies. According to Eyre, the context provided a solution to the problem of Margaret's lengthy diatribes: 'All the characters had some activity and could group themselves, rather than stand around the throne room while this terrible woman was screaming abuse at them' (Eyre, p. 136). At the conclusion, Richard was left alone; during 'I do the wrong and first begin to brawl' (ll. 324ff.), his 'activity' was to extinguish each of the three candelabras. In an arch touch, McKellen exploited the homonym 'whet/wet' ('and withal whet me / To be reveng'd', ll. 332–3, wetted his fingers and pinched out a flame for each of his rivals, 'Rivers, Dorset, Grey'. Once again, the action implied, the lights were going out all over Europe. The emphasis on illumination and extinguishment ran throughout the production. A sinister motif of struck matches flaring up in darkness emerged: at the end of the Scrivener's speech, an upstage match-striking alerted us to the presence of the two thugs who then swooped downstage to jostle the whistle-blowing Scrivener off to a violent end.

This, then, was the world in which McKellen's Richard bustled. Or rather, strode purposefully. In a direct riposte to Sher's athletic, ostentatious assumption of disability, McKellen's deformity was slight, often near-invisible: a small hump, chronic alopecia on his head, and a paralysed left arm. Cheated only of ambidexterity, McKellen's physical accomplishment was a matter less of the grand gesture (e.g. Sher fixing Buckingham's head between his crutches like two mandibles), more of the studied, naturalistic detail: removing and rebuttoning clothes with Lady Anne, extracting and lighting untipped Pall Mall cigarettes, uncorking a bottle of wine on the Eve

of Bosworth, all single-handedly. But it was above all McKellen's
voice that carried much of the characterization. A clipped upper-
class bark learnt on the playing fields of Eton and Sandhurst, it simultaneously conveyed financial privilege and emotional deprivation.
(Some American reviewers found the accent alienating and even
incomprehensible: when the production toured to Brooklyn, John
Heilpern suggested that baffled New Yorkers would have appreciated
'a simultaneous translation' to make sense of such sounds as '*Eeey em
nawt een thah geeving veyun todayah*', Heilpern, p. 167.) McKellen largely
under-played the role's potential for delighted hypocrisy and charismatic complicity with the audience. As Irving Wardle approvingly
noted:

> No one has ever dared to play Richard like this as it involves a total sacri-
> fice of audience sympathy. Instead of a satanically charming ironist, with
> whom the spectator secretly identifies, there is a rigidly banal killer whose
> only distinguishing mark is the grim pursuit of power. He gets no fun out
> of it. Think of the famous laugh lines. 'He cannot live – I hope.' That is no
> joke for McKellen, but a terrified whisper.   (*The Independent*, 27 July 1990)

McKellen generally kept the audience at arm's length. At the close of
Act III, scene v, for example, he told us in joyless and business-like
fashion of his intention 'to give notice that no manner of person / At
any time have recourse unto the princes' (III.v.103–4). Although this
is an exit line, McKellen inventively placed a long pause after the final
word, as if Richard was unsure of whether to flesh out this hint and
let us in on his plans for the princes. The pause was blank, unnerv-
ingly retentive. The decision to then quickly exit confirmed that
Richard did not trust us or need our love enough to risk this act of
confidentiality. It was fitting that this grim anti-hero should not die
in heroic single combat, but be collectively purged by a moral majority. The fight director John Waller is quoted in the production's 'bible'
as advising the cast:

> During the fight, all be aware that Richard is like a wild boar surrounded
> by hounds waiting for the hunter to finish him off. Keep tense and when
> Richmond is in danger close in to help, when he recovers, back off.
> (National Theatre Archive)

The circle of Richmond's troops finally closed in and Richard was communally skewered. Before a climactic death rattle, McKellen repeated 'A horse, a horse, my kingdom for a horse'. As Potter notes: 'Earlier it had been a practical expression of need; now it was addressed, not to anyone on stage, but to a private dream world populated, perhaps, by the Wagnerian Valkyries, perhaps the famous horses of the chivalric heroes of the past' (Potter, 1990, pp. 147–8).

Shakespeare's play began its stage life with a charged relationship with the monarchy. Richmond was, of course, the grandfather of Elizabeth I and it is not surprising that the character is most obviously played as a model of courage and devout sincerity. Richard Eyre's production, almost exactly four centuries later, offered something like a photo-negative of this encomium to the reigning monarch. By foregrounding the Nazi sympathies of some factions of the British Establishment in the 1930s, the production could not help but remind its audience of the shadowy politics of the present Queen's uncle, King Edward VIII. In the early 1590s, Shakespeare would have lost his livelihood if not his life for suggesting that some branches of the royal family tree were rotten. At the close of the twentieth century, however, an analogous suggestion did not cause too much dismay at Buckingham Palace: in January 1991, six months into the run of *Richard III*, Ian McKellen was made a Knight of the British Empire in the New Year's Honours List.

Key Performances: Conclusion

As Huckleberry Finn drifts down the Mississippi, he falls in with the duke, that great huckster-showman who brings mongrel Shakespeare, tipsy lectures on temperance, and examples of 'yellocution' to one-horse towns in the 'State of Arkansaw'. On lean-to shacks and rickety fences he sticks his bills:

> Shakspearean Revival!!!
> Wonderful attraction
> For One Night Only!
> . . .

The thrilling, masterly, and blood-curdling
Broad-sword conflict
In Richard III. !!!
Richard III . . . . Mr. Garrick.
Richmond . . . . Mr. Kean.

There is something poignant and tantalizing about the fantasy of
being able to set these great actors, David Garrick (died 1779) and
Edmund Kean (born *c*.1787), side by side in a 'wonderful attraction'.
Like all theatre, it is a fraud. But, just as the Witches offer Macbeth
'lies like truth' (V.v.42), so the duke's con-man casting has its own
revelatory implications. First, the duke's revival suggests that performance involves not only impersonation of pre-scripted 'characters'
but often also impersonations of other actors. Secondly, it suggests
that in the false spectacle of Kean's Richmond fighting (and defeat-
ing) Garrick's Richard we have a symbolic representation of inter-
generational competition, the quasi-Oedipal struggle of the younger
actor to erase the memory of his predecessor and win the public's
love.

It is appropriate that the anecdotal history of a play so full of
dissimulation, hypocrisy and theatricality should begin with
Manningham's account of the randy Shakespeare ('William the
Conqueror') usurping the place reserved for Burbage's Richard III. It
seems that only one actor at a time can triumph as Richard, can wield
the affective power over the audience so obviously symbolized by
Shakespeare's carnality with the Citizen's wife. As we have seen, the
stage history of *Richard III* is full of such acts of impersonation: Cibber
playing Richard in the style of Sandford, Hackett obsessively recording then reproducing Kean's performance, Olivier putting on the
nasal voice of old actors impersonating Irving. But this acceptance of
tradition is counterpointed by its opposite: the anxiety of influence,
the pressure each new lead actor and director feels to make it new
and disown, even defeat their predecessors. In *Confessions of an Actor*,
Olivier wrote in detail on Burbage, Garrick, Kean, and Irving,
concluding with the wish 'Let me make the judges think that I am the
best bull in the ring' (p. 65). When Antony Sher played Richard he
was recurrently haunted by the spectre of the best bull; one night he

dreamt he saw 'Olivier's face in extreme close-up. Viewing it in a slow circle, closer and closer, till I realise it's not on a cinema screen as I thought, nor carved on the side of a mountain as it next appears, but it's actually *there*. Circling the giant. Closer and closer it comes . . .' (Sher, p. 135). In turn, following the success of Sher and Alexander, Ian McKellen and Richard Eyre waged a more-or-less conscious battle with the memory of their predecessors' production. In the early nineteenth century, Charles Lamb wrote of how:

> Our curiosity is excited, when a *new Hamlet* or a *new Richard* makes his appearance, in the first place, to inquire, how he acted in the *Closet scene*, in the *Tent scene*; how he looked, and how he started, when the *Ghost* came on, and how he cried
>
> Off with his head. So much for Buckingham.
>
> We do not reprehend this minute spirit of comparison. On the contrary, we consider it as a delightful artifice, by which we connect the recreations of the past with those of the present generation, what pleased our fathers with what pleases us.   (Lamb, 1968, p. 18)

Although a source of anxiety for the performer, comparison provides pleasure for the theatregoer. As long as *Richard III* remains one of Shakespeare's most frequently revived plays, this delightful artifice, the opportunity to weigh and contrast a succession of performers and productions, will continue to excite our curiosity. *Richard III* is a history play, but that history is not only that of medieval England, but of the theatre itself.

Coda: Scenes from the Afterlife

Shakespeare's play was not only the product of many texts and a variety of sources, it has itself produced and inspired an enormous array of adaptations, parodies and off-shoots, which have flashed around the edges of the play's mainstream of performance history. Phrases from *Richard III* are known and quoted by people who are often unaware of their origin – how would the British refer to the

months in 1978–9 of industrial strikes and economic depression
without Shakespeare's resonant compound 'winter of [our] discontent'? Intentional allusion and appropriation can be subtle and local.
Charles Dickens's description of Mrs Pipchin in *Dombey and Son*, for
example, highlights the ways in which Richard's physical deformity
has influenced other writers in the vein of the comic grotesque:

> This celebrated Mrs Pipchin was a marvellous ill-favoured, ill-condi-
> tioned old lady, of a stooping figure, with a mottled face, like bad marble,
> a hook nose, and a hard grey eye, that looked as if it might have been
> hammered at on an anvil without sustaining any injury.

'Marvellous ill-favoured' is, of course, how Shakespeare describes the
appearance of Richard and Buckingham at the opening of Act III,
scene v; the stooping figure and hook nose seem to follow by association and anticipate not only Shaw's comparison of Richard with
Punch, but also Olivier's extravagant proboscis. The imagery and
language of *Richard III* thus insinuate their way into the texture of
novels, poems, journalism and advertising.

On a more expansive level, the play has, for over three hundred
years, generated further pieces of theatre. In Bertolt Brecht's satiric
parable *The Resistible Rise of Arturo Ui* (1941), *Richard III* is invoked as a
dramaturgical model for Hitler's ascent to power. Ui (Hitler) is head
gangster in Chicago (Germany), profiting from a protection racket
on the city's food suppliers. In order to expand his empire, he orders
the murder of Ignatius Dullfeet, a thinly disguised portrait of the
Austrian Chancellor Engelbert Dollfuss. His widow Betty Dullfeet's
submission thus becomes symbolic of Austria's surrender to Nazi
'protection'. The wooing scene between Ui and Betty is closely
modelled on that between Richard and Anne. Ui accosts Betty as she
leaves her husband's funeral and, with hypocritical panache, exploits
the rawness of her grief. The scene concludes:

BETTY, *feebly*   You won't succeed.
UI   I will. That much I know.
BETTY   From this protector God protect us!

[cf. *Richard III*, IV.i.14–15]

UI   Give
    Me your answer.
        He holds out his hand.
                    Is it friendship?
BETTY   Never while I live!
                    Cringing with horror, she runs out.
                                        (Brecht, pp. 205–6)

Despite her hasty and appalled exit, in the play's final scene she has relented and is advising the citizens of Cicero (Austria) to place their trust in Ui. Playful echoes of *Richard III* (and *Julius Caesar*) continue in the next scene when Ui, 'plagued by a nightmare', is haunted by the ghost of one of his victims. Earlier in the play, Ui is instructed by a Shakespearian actor in the art of successful public speaking.

Arturo Ui represents one of the most successful appropriations of Shakespeare's play, a riff that has fed back into *Richard*'s stage history by inspiring productions, like that of Richard Eyre, that have drawn analogies between the events of the play and the rise of fascism in Europe in the 1930s. The following extracts offer brief further glimpses into the play's fruitful alternative afterlife and bear testimony to the continuing cultural fascination with Shakespeare's irresistible comic-villain.

1   From 'The Rise and Fall of Richard III; or, A New Front to an Old
     Dicky: A Richardsonian Burlesque' (1868) by F. C. Burnand

Burnand's skit is one of many parodies of the play written in the nineteenth century and produced with the sole intention of making an audience laugh. The scene: Old Holborn Valley, near the Bishop of Ely's Strawberry Gardens. Richard bets Buckingham, Catesby and Tyrrell 'sixteen (bad) half-crowns to one' that Anne will accept him. She enters and the four men join her in a song which attempts to diagnose her unhappiness. These inserted airs are common in nineteenth-century burlesques and, when reprinted, help to convey some of the variety-show quirkiness of these events.

ANNE   [singing to the tune of the 'Gambling Chorus from Roberto le Diable']

> Oh dear! oh dear! Oh! what a sad existence!
> To sleep, to weep, to weep away the day;
> To get, to get, a very small subsistence,
> Living in a very, very miserable way.

TYRRELL AND CATESBY   (*coming forward*)

    How do you do?

    How do you do?

ANNE   Not very well, well, well, thank you.

FOUR MEN   {We're sorry to hear that of you.

ANNE   {I'm sorry to say that to you.

FOUR MEN   And what hurts you?

    Is it your shoe?

    Is it your

ANNE   'Tis not my shoe, shoe, shoe, shoe, shoe?

FOUR MEN   I wish we knew (*da capo*).

ANNE   Oh pooh! pooh! pooh! (*da capo*).

FOUR MEN   Or an attack,

ANNE   No, no attack.

ANNE AND THE FOUR   Alack!

    Lumbago? Back?

FOUR MEN   Send for a quack.

ANNE   I want no quack.

ALL   Quack, quack, &c.

THE FOUR   Not want a quack?

ANNE   Don't want a quack.

    Quack, quack, &c. (*to the end.*)

RICHARD   You're pretty well, I hope?

ANNE   Hump back! *avaunt!*

RICHARD   I *vant* to speak to you, and so I shan't.

ANNE   Don't cross my path, you monster of deformities!

    You most enourmousest of all enormities.

RICHARD   I see that you a passion for me foster.

ANNE   Passion for you! *High, mighty, double Gloster.*

RICHARD   Oh, call me double Gloster, if you please,

    As long as I, in your eyes, am the cheese.

ANNE   A cheese! Why then I cut you. (*Going to* R[ichard], *he stops her.*)

RICHARD   I've the daring

    To ask you to consider this cheese *paring.*

ANNE   You are hump-backed.

RICHARD   Oh, hump-bug!

ANNE   And knock knee'd.

RICHARD   A friend *in-knee'd*, maam, is a friend in deed.

ANNE   You killed my pa'in law.

RICHARD   Then kill me too.

    (*She offers at him with parasol, and he winces.*)

    Don't tickle! What's a pa'in law to you?

ANNE   My husband too – Do you deny the crime?

RICHARD   No. But don't hit me quite so hard next time.

    'Twas for your love: now kill me with a frown.

    (*She is about to strike him; he winces.*)

    You wouldn't strike a fellow when he's down.

    Ah, what a hand! And what an eye! (*Aside.*) So green.

    (*Aloud.*) – Be mine and you shall be all England's Queen.

ANNE   Upon your word.

RICHARD   And honour. Yes?

ANNE   Well, yes;

    You *do* get round one so I must confess.

    You've shewn that what I thought were your duplicities

    And crimes, were –

RICHARD   Pardonable eccentricities.

BUCKINGHAM   Richard, well done. A 'yes' from her you've forced.

RICHARD   Good. Now you'll pay all those half-crowns you lost.

2   *The Final Moments of the Rustavelli Theatre Company's 'Richard III' (as staged at The Roundhouse, London, 1980)*

The production programme listed some of the changes the company had made in adapting the text. This is how the production ended. After Elizabeth's exit and Richard's 'Relenting fool, and shallow, changing woman!' Richard was cursed by his mother, concluding with 'Shame serves thy life and doth thy death attend' (IV.iv.185). Richmond and Margaret were on stage throughout the play. After Richard called for a horse, he and Richmond fought in strange single combat wearing huge maps of England which engulfed the antagonists like tents.

RICHARD   O coward conscience, how dost thou afflict me!

    The lights burn blue. It is now dead midnight.

MARGARET   So now prosperity begins to mellow
       And drop into the rotten mouth of death.
RICHARD   Cold fearful drops stand on my trembling flesh.
MARGARET   At hand, at hand,
       Ensues his piteous and unpitied end –
RICHARD   What do I fear? Myself? There's none else by.
       Richard loves Richard – that is, I am I.
       Is there a murderer here?
MARGARET   Yes, thou art! Fly!
RICHARD   What, from myself?
MARGARET   Lest thou revenge!
RICHARD   Myself upon myself?
       Alack, I love myself. Wherefore? For any good
MARGARET   That thou thyself hast done unto thyself.
RICHARD   Hush!
MARGARET   There is no creature loves thee
       And if thou die, no soul will pity thee.
RICHARD   Nay, wherefore should they, since that I myself
       Find in myself no pity to myself?
JESTER   The death of King Richard III.
RICHMOND   O Thou, whose captain I account myself,
       Look on my forces with a gracious eye;
       Put in their hands Thy bruising irons of wrath,
       That they may crush down with a heavy fall
       The wretched, bloody, and usurping boar –
RICHARD   Richmond, can an ungrateful brat as thou art
       Grab the throne of England?
RICHMOND   God and our good cause fight upon our side;
       The prayers of holy saints and wronged souls,
       Like high-reared bulwarks, stand before our faces.
RICHARD   Conscience is but a word that cowards use,
       Devised at first to keep the strong in awe.
       Our strong arms be our conscience, swords our law!
RICHMOND   A bloody tyrant and a homicide;
       One raised in blood, and one in blood
       Established; those whom we fight against
       Had rather have us win than him they follow.
RICHARD   Much thou knowest brat, bastard
       They'll pray for thee, but die for me.
       A horse! A horse! My kingdom for a horse!

3   From 'Ten Oorlog' (1997) by Tom Lanoye

Ten Oorlog (*To War*) is the Flemish playwright Tom Lanoye's adaptation of Shakespeare's eight history plays from *Richard II* to *Richard III*. Directed by Luk Perceval, the 11-hour staging of the play was first performed in Flanders in 1997 and has since played to great acclaim in Austria, Germany and Switzerland. Witty, brutal and iconoclastic, Lanoye combines his native Flemish with French and a flexible English that ranges from Shakespeare's own words to a demotic argot reminiscent of *A Clockwork Orange* and the films of Quentin Tarantino. Conceived as an allegory on power and the need for survival, Lanoye's adaptations of Shakespeare's plays also make a more specific critique of society and politics in Belgium at the end of the twentieth century. This is how he translates, abridges and adapts Richard's opening encounter with Clarence (I.ii.42–116).

RISJAAR   Yo, bruur!
What's up? Why is the King z'n bruur   *the King's brother*
   gevangen,   *prisoner*
As in a chain-gang, closely supervised?
SJORS   Edwaar is so concerned about me that
He sends me naar de fokking Toren, bruur/   *the fucking Tower*
RISJAAR   Oh no! But why?
SJORS   Because my name is Sjors.
RISJAAR   But how insane – you're not to blame for that.
Waar ligt het echte paard gebonden?   *Where's the real horse*
   Shoot!   *tied up [Dutch*
                                                                 proverb: Who's really
                                                                 to blame?]

SJORS   Hij zweert bij waarzeggers en   *He swears by prophets*
   wichelaars,   *and soothsayers*
He reads in stars, in clouds, in guts of geese, and
Kiest dan de letter 'G' iut 't apfabet   *Chooses then the letter 'G'*
Because a witch predicted him dat 'G'   *from the alphabet*
Zijn zonen zal onterven, alletwee.   *Will disinherit his sons,*
                                                                 both of them

RISJAAR   Of course: You're 'George' Niet   *[Sjors is short for George*
   'Sjors'; jaja, natúúrlijk.   *in Dutch]*

SJORS   And because 'George', my name, begins met 'G',

Ben ik de klos, ben ik plots de risee.   *I'm the idiot, suddenly the joker*

RISJAAR   Zo gaat dat, when the bitch   *That's how it goes when*
commands de vent.   *the bitch commands the bloke*

't Is niet mijn bruur u die Toren instuurt,   *It's not my brother that's*
It is his bitch who makes him spit on you.   *sending you to the*
We are not safe here, bruur, not fokking safe.   *Tower*

SJORS   Geen mens, geen hond or he is in   *No person, nor dog*
big danger

Unless he is related aan die teef.   *. . . to that bitch*

RISJAAR   Since our bruur is married met that widow

Groeit heel haar nest van mus tot   *Her whole nest grows*
mighty sparrow   *from sparrow to*

En wordt de wet gemaakt door hún   *And the law is made by*
gekwetter.   *their twittering.*

BEWAKER   Nobele heren, ik smeek u,   *Noble gentlemen, I beg*
vergeef me   *you, forgive me,*

Maar zijne hoogheid the King heft verboden   *But his highness has forbidden*

Dat wie dan ook, van welke rang of stand,   *Anyone, of whatever rank or standing,*

Onder vier ogen met zijn broer zou praten.   *To talk privately with your brother.*

SJORS   You got your orders, pal, we will obey.

RISJAAR   We fokking have to, we are the rejected,

The fok-offparia's van deze Queen.   *The fuck-off pariahs of this Queen*

Vaarwel, m'n bruur. Ik haasr mij naar   *Farewell, brother, I haste*
the King   *me to the King*

En welke shit ik ook voor u moet slikken –   *And whatever shit I have to swallow for you –*

If necessary, even kiss the bitch –

I'll do it, aals ik jou maar vrij kan lullen.   *. . . if only I can talk you free of this.*

Just one more thing: dat bruurs elkaar   *that brothers screw around*
zó kloten?   *with each other like this*

It hurts me, man, much dieper dan you think.

    (kust hem, huilend)   *(kisses him, crying)*

SJORS   I know that neither of us like it, bruur.

RISJAAR   I cross my heart:

    You will not bite the dust in dat cachot.   *that hellhole*

    I'll take your pains and chains on me, I'll free ya –

    It won't take long, geduld!   *patience*

SJORS   I have no choice.

5 The Play on Screen

In the early decades of the twentieth century, at the moment when the stage had widely restored Shakespeare's texts and when actors such as Sir Henry Irving were finally perceived as legitimate enough to be awarded a knighthood, a fresh threat emerged to this newly sanctified mode of representation. Suddenly in the new palladium of pleasure that was the picture house, a paying audience could dispense with the live actor entirely. As one of Shakespeare's most popular plays, it was a small matter of time before *Richard III* made the leap from stage to screen. This chapter offers brief introductions to each of the six twentieth-century versions of the play most widely available to the viewer.

Explicable Dumb-shows: Benson (1910) and Warde (1912)

Two silent film accounts of *Richard III* survive and are commercially available thanks to the labours of the American and British Film Institutes. The first, a 1910, eleven-minute canter starring Sir Frank Benson, is of more interest as a record of a piece of theatre than as cinema. Filmed in the Memorial Theatre, Stratford-upon-Avon, from a doggedly fixed camera somewhere in the middle stalls, it records heightened moments from Benson's stage production while only once (with the use of dissolves in the ghost scene) exploiting filmic techniques. To the uninitiated, the succession of scenes must have been confusing; perhaps it served as an extended trailer, tempting them into the theatre to see if *Richard III* made any more sense there. Robert Hamilton Ball, quoting Tyrrell, calls the film a 'most arch deed of piteous slaughter' (p. 84), but there are moments of interest. The production rushes in where even Cibber feared to tread, not merely reporting, but showing the stabbing of Prince Edward in the aftermath of the Battle of Tewkesbury. The wooing of Lady Anne is clearly an exercise in mesmerism; as she turns to leave, Richard's outstretched arm sucks her back into his magnetic field; he even forces her hand to levitate to a height convenient for ring-placing. The film is worth seeing for a glimpse into the ways Richard's villainy was characterized. The disability is slight, as evidenced by the remarkably athletic removal of King Henry's body from the Tower: Richard turns, hitches the corpse's legs over his shoulders, grips the knees then marches out with King Henry staring back, upside down, a singularly dangerous exit that might have broken either man's back; perhaps Benson recalled Richard's aside in *3 Henry VI*, 'This shoulder was ordained so thick to heave; / And heave it shall some weight or break my back' (V.vii.23–4). Richard's callous brutality is revealed in the council scene when, having doomed Hastings, he picks up an apple (which he himself has placed on stage for just such a contingency) and exits chomping and shaking with mirth. Richard may not dine before he sees Hastings's head, but in Benson he allows himself a snack.

Only two years separate Benson's and James Keane's versions, but the results seem decades apart. Discovered in an Oregon basement in 1996, Keane's film starring Frederick B. Warde is the oldest surviving American feature film. (A feature film is technically defined as one that consists of four or more reels, each reel running to approximately ten minutes.) In 1912, advertisements were posted for 'The Gigantic 5,000ft. Feature Film' – never mind the quality, feel the length – a five-reeler in which, as a later programme boasted, 1500 people and 200 horses had participated in '5 Distinct Battle Scenes' (Rothwell, 2000, p. 35). The blurb was accurate about the number of fights, if not the human and equine resources at the director's disposal. A huge sum, $30,000, had been lavished on this treatment and the result is remarkable. Frederick Warde was sixty-one when he played Richard on film. Born in England in the year of the Great Exhibition, he had emigrated to the States, acted in Booth's company, subsequently formed his own, and now found himself a leading man in a miraculous new medium. A veteran of the Chautauqua circuit, he was no stranger to story-telling. It was, then, part of the film's appeal that Warde would introduce and lecture on the piece in person. The opening of the film, astonishingly, recognizes this framing device: there is Warde, a tweedy professor, pince-nez pinched between finger and thumb, bowing his acknowledgements to the movie theatre audience. What follows is fifty minutes of Shakespeare heavily filtered through both Cibber and the nascent technology of the cinema. In strong contrast to Benson, the use of outdoor and indoor settings is varied and impressive, perhaps most so when we see Richmond's handsome three-mast boat hove into 'Milford Haven'. The amount and detail of plot conveyed is equally sophisticated, leading, in one instance, to the unforgettable title card: 'Prophesy of wizard thrown in at window'. We are also shown such non-textual but plot-elucidating moments as Richard forcing the quill into the hands of the dying Edward to sign Clarence's death warrant, Richard's wooing of Princess Elizabeth, and the subsequent poisoning of a bed-ridden Anne by a lackey physician.

The film starts, like Benson's, at Tewkesbury and then proceeds to Richard murdering Henry in the Tower, repeating with variation the sadistic business of re-stabbing the King after he is dead and running his finger down the bloody blade. Warde, like Benson (and many Richards since, including McKellen), celebrates the end of Act III, scene vii by tossing his Bible sky-high and raising his right arm in triumph. Far from the dignified *éminence grise* glimpsed in the prologue, Warde's Richard stomps about, bowing and scraping to his erstwhile superiors and, literally, thigh-slapping after moments of triumph such as Anne's wooing. But there is a genuine chill in the coronation scene: an evidently unhappy court waits, motionless, for his arrival; when crowned he stalks, screen left-to-right, towards the throne with Tarquin's ravishing strides. The film ends on a strikingly downbeat image: the slaughtered Richard lies at the foot of a stone wall strewn with broken weapons and snapped shields – bruisèd arms hung up for monuments.

Perfumed Legend: Olivier (1955)

In 1944–5 and 1948–9 thousands witnessed his Richard on stage; in 1955 millions now saw Olivier's sardonic portrayal on the small and large screen. In America, rights were sold to NBC for a pre-cinema-release television broadcast and an estimated forty million people tuned in. This film ensured that Olivier's mark on the role would forever cut deep. Its vivid coloration defiantly outfaces time and the greying of memory. The opening credits quickly establish the film's attitude to both history and text. First, a long disclaimer throws a sop to the pro-Ricardians by acknowledging Shakespeare's play as based on and perpetuating 'legend' rather than history. History without legends is compared to flowers without perfume, thus preparing us for the pungent and chromatic quality of the film, which, with its Book of Hours appearance, is tonally reminiscent of the earlier *Henry V*. Secondly, Shakespeare's by-line credit is underwritten, if not subverted, by the notice:

With some interpolations
by
David Garrick and Colley Cibber
etc

That 'etc' marks a highly theatrical nonchalance about authorial attribution: the play as it has been proved to work on stage is the thing. Crowd-pleasers such as 'Off with his head; so much for Buckingham' and 'Richard's himself again' (whispered in confidence to his horse, White Surrey) are retained. But more importantly, the cavalier attitude to the textual integrity of *Richard III* is evident throughout, whether in the highly creative inter-splicings and rearrangements of scene sections, and the inclusion of lines from *3 Henry VI*, or, say, in the prominent position given to Mistress Shore, who is a knowing presence throughout the first half of the film. Olivier's account of the virtuoso filming and delivery of Richard's first soliloquy nicely captures the film's ambivalence to the play-text: 'Even thinking about the way I shot the soliloquy fills me with pleasure: *ideas springing naturally from the text (which, admittedly, I had manipulated)* and from the main idea of having Richard speak directly to the camera' (Olivier, 1986, p. 304; my italics). Whose text is it anyway? That Richard-like mischievous parenthetical aside reveals that beneath the loyal professions of textual fidelity lurks the cinematic usurper, ever ready to be unfaithful to his playwright King if the effect creates sensation in the viewer.

Olivier's film has the confidence and lack of neurosis with which mid-1950s, post-Coronation England at least wished to view itself. The opening minutes of the film include a coronation procession in which an earlier Elizabeth bestows regal waves on her adoring subjects, a coincidence that must have rekindled some very recent memories. Confidence also sprang from the sheer calibre of Olivier's cast. When the crown is placed on Edward's (Sir Cedric Hardwicke) head, Sir Laurence glances meaningfully across to Buckingham (Sir Ralph Richardson), who in turn catches the eye of Clarence (Sir John Gielgud): in a matter of seconds, the film is legitimated, four-fold, by nothing less than the royal seal of approval. (The casting also enables at least one in-joke: when Richard tells the murderers not to dally with their victim 'for Clarence is well-spoken', Olivier seems to be aware of the colossal understatement: in the event, Gielgud is bundled off without ceremony, Olivier the director sardonically cutting his extended imploring and reducing the voice beautiful to a death scream.) The cast move within a *mise-en-scène* that centres on a large chamber defined only by the throne and the bodies within it. Windows and doors allow the camera – usually under Richard's effective direction – to peep in and out of this symbolic space. The casting of Richard's shadow forms another motif, as do the musical signatures and variations of William Walton's score. Situations such as Clarence's death or most notably the wooing of Anne are decompressed and spread out over two scenes in the interests of suspense and psychological plausibility. Other sequences concentrate and conflate events to serve narrative explication and intensification. Outside Clarence's cell, Catesby and Buckingham deliver the reprieve to Richard, while the ubiquitous Mistress Shore arrives to greet the 'newly-delivered' Hastings, prompting Buckingham to inveigh against the 'night-walking heralds', remarks which she overhears. When Richard sanctimoniously censures Edward for having 'overmuch consumed his royal person' (I.i.140) he glances reproachfully at Shore. While most of the text from this scene is taken from Act I, scene i (with some additions by 'etc'), it occurs almost a third of the way through the film, where it better suits Olivier's purpose.

Only with the depiction of Bosworth Field does the film break from the studio locations of royal chamber, walkways and courtyards.

Bosworth is surprisingly unEnglish: a parched plain overlooked by arid semi-mountains. The ghosts, appearing only to Richard, materialize from a luminous miasma in the semi-distance of the field. Showing what Shakespeare could not, Olivier also conveys the military logistics and the decisive desertion of Stanley. In the face of these odds, Richard's incursion appears solitary and suicidal. His death, a mass ritual slaughter of the scapegoated scourge of God, further emphasizes the inevitability of retribution. The battle was filmed on a bull farm in southern Spain, using soldiers from General Franco's army, who came cheap as extras. The irony of this has passed largely unnoticed. That soldiers living under and serving a military dictatorship established in the aftermath of civil war should be fictionally delivering medieval England from such a tyrant is a depressing reflection both of the unethical nature of outsourced jobs and of the historical recurrence of military *coups*.

Finally, it is the image and the sound of Olivier's performance that continues to cast its spell. Among other sources of inspiration, he claimed he was impersonating the impersonations of old actors 'doing' Irving (see Chapter 4: Key Productions and Performances). It is apt that Olivier's own performance has spawned countless imitations and representations, from Salvador Dali's portrait of the double-mask of actor and character to Peter Sellars's inspired rendition of the Beatles' 'A Hard Day's Night', in which the rhyme of 'working like a dog' and 'sleeping like a log' cast an unexpected new light on the insomniac villain at whom dogs bark. Thanks to celluloid, Olivier's performance, the brilliantly executed apotheosis of Cibber's vision, will remain to entertain 'the time to come' (IV.iv.308).

Bard on the Beeb: Howell (1983)

Jane Howell's production of *Richard III* for the BBC Shakespeare is unique among the versions discussed here for at least two reasons. First, it was made for television (and video), with all the technical, budgetary and audience imperatives of that medium. Secondly, it is the only screen production of *Richard III* conceived within the context of the entire first tetralogy. (Both the Hall/Barton and Pennington/

Bogdanov *War of the Roses* were shown on television and available on video, but these were filmed versions of stage productions, not made for television.) Howell's tetralogy was screened on four consecutive Sundays in January 1983 – a rare month of Sundays, indeed, for prime-time weekend television programming. Unlike many of the BBC Shakespeares, Howell resisted the cautious and inherently misguided attempts at 'definitive' production, which makes dull watching of so many plays in the series. Her approach also contrasts with that of Richard Loncraine (McKellen's director, discussed below). Whereas he sought to erase the theatrical vestiges of the stage production by converting them into the grammar and conventions of cinema, Howell, conversely, produced fourteen hours of television that aspired to the condition of theatre. It is Howell's and not Loncraine's adaptation that appears as if it were based on an original stage production. Rather than embracing the variety of interior locations afforded by the chameleon space of the television studio, she instead opted for a single, permanent set: a consciously crude wooden structure of split levels, ramps, exposed supports and swinging doors. The governing metaphor was that of the children's playground – she compared the behaviour of the English nobility to that of 'prep school children' (Willis, p. 167) – combined with a generalized medieval aesthetic. She also established a repertory company of actors for the project. '*Richard III* is like a nightmare' she claimed, and Clarence's experience tells us that nightmares are generally more terrifying if we at least start by recognizing the people we meet there. As in a repertory production, actors doubled and trebled roles, once again marking the distance from both television and filmic practices. David Burke, for example, played Humphrey, Duke of Gloucester, Dick the Butcher, then Catesby, a recurrent yes-man in successive regimes. In *Richard III*, Paul Jesson's Clarence reappears as the last of the messengers bringing 'songs of death' (IV.iv.425) to Richard. As with stage tetralogies, images as much as casting resonated across the four plays. In *1 Henry VI*, Ron Cook had played a hunchbacked porter to the French countess, whom Talbot's men had surrounded and tormented. The image would reappear, amplified but familiar, on Bosworth Field, when the same actor's Richard would be surrounded and skewered by another outnumbering circle.

Production in the fuller context of the first tetralogy means, of course, that this version is unique in having no need for an orienting prologue: *3 Henry VI* had ended with a celebratory dance; *Richard* opens with this as noises off. Richard, closing two doors, quickly muffles this so that *his* play may begin: so much for continuity. Throughout the production, when the actors rehearse historical grievances, they seem confident of being understood by a television audience that has, ideally, been following the story as a form of soap opera. As befitting its remit to be not for an age, the BBC Shakespeare tended to use fullish texts. Here Howell seems again to mark her difference from cinematic *Richards* by going still further and cutting nearly nothing (the film runs for almost four hours). As with all stagings of the tetralogy, there is a sense in which Richard's character is diminished. This diminution – some might argue that it is a more accurate proportion – is compounded by a text in which no enemy's or victim's voice goes unheard. Ron Cook's Richard is child-like, plausible and understated: the histrionicism of the part is reined in to suit the prevailing gloom of *Richard III* when played as conclusion to an epic of internecine suffering.

Despite the inevitably governing 'vision' of the director, the production, as Howell obviously wished, belongs to the actors. Her camera work is unobtrusive: she is adept at creating sustained single-camera sequences in which the composition is subtly tweaked and the overall effect is one of fluency. Like Richard moving Anne towards the 'slower method', Howell immediately establishes this tempo in which the basic unit of time is the scene. Close-up camera-address is, naturally, a common device, but it is not Richard's sole prerogative. His cohorts Buckingham and Catesby use it, but so too do Brackenbury, the Second Executioner and Richmond. For an audience accustomed to either director's theatre or the usual foci, rearrangements and abridgements of filmed Shakespeare, Howell's production offers little in the way of ostentatiously 'interpretive' moments. In *Richard III*, obviously directed highlights include the scratching of Ratcliffe's quill at Pomfret as he grimly reaps his way through red tape, and also the Prince of Wales's perspicacious attitude to his sinister uncle. Most memorable of all is the production's closing image. The camera pans up across a mess of bodies, limbs inextricably entwined, a macabre tribute to the ensemble of actors whose work now forms a common body. Atop this pyramid Golgotha, Margaret sits laughing as she cradles Richard's punctured corpse in an inverted pietà.

From Stage to Screen: Loncraine–McKellen (1995)

Three years after his last stage performance as Richard, Ian McKellen starred in the first general-release film version of the play since Olivier's. The central interpretive thrust was carried over from the stage production: the viewer is asked to imagine the plausibility of a fascist *coup* in 1930s England, an England of Oswald Mosley and an Establishment riddled with Nazi sympathizers. Once again, the para-textual apparatus of the interpretation – in this case, McKellen's extensive annotations to his published screenplay – partly claimed and partly disowned the historic specificity: 'Although the film uses the iconography of fascism, Richard is a dictator pure and simple, from neither the right nor the left. The fascistic references are a reminder that an English dictatorship (even by a Royal claimant) is credible within the 1930s setting' (p. 216). Richard Loncraine, an eclectic director whose credits ranged from Dennis Potter's disturbing *Brimstone and Treacle* to the production of roughly four hundred (more consumer-friendly) TV adverts, directed *Richard III* with an opulent panache that remained broadly faithful to Eyre's stage inter-pretation whilst also, through a combination of glamour, knowing-ness and slickness, changing its overall impact on the viewer. The first ten minutes of the film, roughly one-ninth of its playing time, elapses before a Shakespearian word is spoken. A bravura piece of film-making indebted to American *auteurs* such as De Palma or Scorsese, the opening sequence firmly established the piece's cine-matic credentials. As in the stage productions of Michael Bogdanov (1988) and Stephen Pimlott (1995), Richard's soliloquy begins as an after-dinner speech, here snapped off in a cut that takes us from ball-room to bathroom, where, in a conjunction suggestive of sexual impotence, Richard descants on his deformity while draining his bladder.

In keeping with most filmed Shakespeare, approximately 73 per cent of the text is cut. As in Olivier's film, there is no room for Margaret, not surprisingly given the secular, self-contained nature of the overarching interpretation, although some of her lines are redistributed to the Duchess of York. Both Richmond and Princess Elizabeth feature throughout. Queen Elizabeth is rarely seen without her daughter, and, in an interpolated vignette, we see Richmond and the Princess drowsy in morning-after-the-night-before nuptial bliss before Bosworth. Elizabeth's Woodville family becomes American; 'witness', comments McKellen, 'the British Establishment's outcry in 1936, when King Edward VIII wanted Wallis Simpson to be his queen' (p. 54). A new emphasis is thus introduced to her line 'Small joy have I in being *this* country's queen' ('England's queen' in the text, I.iii.110). The male Woodvilles (Rivers, Grey and Dorset) are represented solely by Robert Downey Jr's Rivers, a jaunty playboy with a soft spot for Pan-Am air hostesses.

The film climaxes with a battle scene set in and around Battersea power station. (Stanley's crucial defection is marked by an RAF bombing raid.) 'A horse, a horse' is prompted by Richard's jeep wheel-spinning in patriotic mud. Chased by Richmond up and along the bomb-blasted skeleton of the edifice, Richard finds himself tottering on a precarious ledge. Richmond is primed to shoot, when the tyrant chooses to fall back into the hell-fire behind him. The penultimate shot of the film is a close-up of the next king smiling with sinister conceit directly into camera, a mode of address that has hitherto been exclusively Richard's privilege. In Eyre's production, Richmond had suggested nervousness, an incipient inability to lead, but nothing implied this Kottian reading. On film, we have a cinematic rendering of Kott's closing image of the Grand Mechanism: 'Henry VII speaks of peace, forgiveness, justice. And suddenly he gives a crowing sound like Richard's, and, for a second, the same sort of grimace twists his face. The bars are being lowered. The face of the new king is radiant again' (p. 46). Loncraine's film insistently marks its distance from the stage through a variety of filmic allusions. Rivers's *in flagrente* death, skewered from beneath a groaning mattress, places us firmly in the slasher-flick genre, while the scream of his one-night stand merges with that of a train whistle in a direct quotation of Hitchcock's *The Thirty-Nine Steps*. Richard's final descent into the inferno evokes Slim Pickens's plummet strapped to an Atom bomb in *Dr Strangelove*. Simultaneously, the use of Al Jolson's 'I'm sitting on top of the world' recalls James Cagney's fiery self-destruction in *White Heat*, and his climactic boast, 'Made it, Ma, top of the world!'

Streetwise Shakespeare: Pacino's quest (1996)

At the beginning of the twentieth century, Frederick Warde, understandably fearing that silent performance cannot speak for itself, became both actor and commentator. At the end of the century in the same city in which Warde's film was shot, another actor was feeling anxious about presenting his Richard to an uncomprehending audience. Al Pacino's solution was to share. In a move that was both post-modern and entirely befitting the psycho-analytic bent of the city in which he grew up, Pacino made a film about a film of a play, a film in which anxieties could be aired and discussed, not repressed. The result is a quest: *Looking for Richard*. Pacino had played Richard twice before on stage (1973 and 1979). Rather than competing with the cinematic shade of Olivier, he chose to embed fully produced excerpts within a collage of interviews, rehearsals and interpretive pow-wows. The film explores three main themes: (1) How does an actor find the truth and authentic feeling in Shakespeare? (2) Are American actors at a disadvantage compared with their British counterparts? (3) What does Shakespeare mean to the average American? For Pacino – and perhaps American actors more generally – the quest for emotional honesty and motivational plausibility is everything, a sacred aim learned at the knee of Lee Strasberg or any one of the post-Stanislavskian gurus who oversaw the training of Pacino's generation of actors.

The film has been labelled 'aggressively postcolonial' by at least one critic (Cartelli, p. 194) in that it attempts to appropriate Shakespeare for America and wrestle ownership away from English heritage sites, scholars' studies and the voice-beautiful of Anglo-Shakespearian acting. It does so with great wit and not a little contrivance. In one sequence, Pacino and co-director Frederick Kimball visit Shakespeare's Birthplace apparently expecting a score of epiphanies. Unmoved, they choose instead to goof off, sending-up their own status as American tourists, and like Bill and Ted's, their 'excellent adventure' ends in bathos. Elsewhere, to illustrate how little we can learn from scholars, they cut to Oxford academic Emrys Jones to ask why Richard wants to marry Anne. He admits he's not exactly sure and the camera pans to a dumbfounded Pacino and a satisfied Kimball, who, in the previous scene, has bawled at his anxious leading man: 'You know more about Richard III than any fucking scholar!' If these moments confidently undermine British authority, at other points the film is not so cocksure. Emyrs Jones and Barbara Everett were clearly chosen as much for their almost parodic scholarly appearances – owl-like, bespectacled, fashion-unconscious – as for their intellectual authority. Nevertheless their contributions are on the whole illuminating, and respected as such by Pacino. Similarly, the anti-climactic trip to the Birthplace is counterpointed by Pacino's pilgrimage to the semi-built Globe theatre, where he only partially mocks his own shrine-worshipping. For a truly postcolonial film, too much respect is also accorded the parade of British Shakespearian actors who, with varying degrees of condescension, ruminate on why Americans are so scared of acting Shakespeare.

The performance sequences, too, fall into a double-bind. On the one hand, the camera finds (and helps create) fresh, unforced and 'truthful' moments of the type Pacino was presumably 'looking for'. On the other, the film's commitment to popularization through informality is compromised: the sumptuous costumes, medieval settings, the liturgically swelling soundtrack all implicitly confirm the cliché that playing Shakespeare 'properly' involves old world clothing and locations. The performances are just as engaging – and perhaps more so for the putative man-in-the-New-York-street whom Pacino seeks to enthuse – when played in rehearsal clothes and spaces: Pacino might have here looked to Louis Malle's *Vanya on 42nd Street* (1994) for inspiration. Cutting quickly between talking heads, vox pops, documentary, mocumentary, rehearsal log, and costume drama, it is not always clear what Pacino's film is searching for or what we are looking at. The combination of performance, process, and commentary anticipates the packed menu of the commercial DVD format or the range of the hypertextual experience. But if its aims are often confused, *Looking for Richard* consistently stimulates and provokes, and seems an appropriately experimental, exploratory coda to the twentieth-century's attempts to transpose *Richard III* from the 'wooden O' (*Henry V*, Prologue, l. 13) to the silver screen.

6 Critical Assessments

What William Hazlitt observed two hundred years ago remains true today: '*Richard III* may be considered as properly a stage-play: it belongs to the theatre, rather than the closet' (1916, p. 187). Nevertheless, as was remarked in Chapter 1, *Richard III* was frequently reprinted in Shakespeare's own lifetime and was clearly popular with readers. Since then a fair amount of ink has been spilt and brains tossed about in the attempt to understand what the play might mean, what Shakespeare intended when he wrote it, and what we as readers and viewers should understand this phenomenal stage vehicle as signifying in the realms of politics, history, morality and psychology. This chapter offers a selective, chronological account of the history of the play's criticism. While interpretive concerns have evolved and mutated, there are many enduring dilemmas: How should we respond to the combination of evil and attractiveness in Richard? How, if at all, can his villainy be explained? Should the play be viewed on its own or as part of a four-, eight- or even ten-part cycle of history plays? Equally consistently, the history of interpretation attests to the difficulty of separating critical from stage history, as many, especially pre-twentieth-century critics are responding to both Shakespeare's text and its latest reincarnation on stage. Above all, critical responses over the centuries confirm the great truism of interpretation: that the personal and historical context of the critic inescapably influences criticism. As we will see, the responses of such diverse figures as Lord Byron, Sigmund Freud, George Bernard Shaw, E. M. W. Tillyard and Jan Kott to *Richard III* can all be understood through (if not fully explained by) knowledge of their historical and personal circumstances. In the last half-century, debate has been dominated by the politics of historiography. Is *Richard III* the culmination of Shakespeare's attempt to justify the ways of God to men? Did, as E. M. W. Tillyard claimed, every sentence of Richmond's closing speech raise 'the Elizabethans to an ecstasy of feeling'? (p. 207). Or conversely, does Shakespeare in this and other history plays interrogate the very notion of authority? Is the struggle for power, as Jan Kott argues, 'always stripped of all mythology [as] a struggle for the crown, between people who have a name, a title and power?' (p. 7). And yet we run before our horse to market. For most of the critical history of the play, individual psychology rather than historico-political intention has been the dominant theme of written responses to the play.

Richard before the Romantics

The first piece of criticism that probably alludes to Shakespeare's play was circulated in manuscript form in the early sixteenth century and then reprinted in Sir William Cornwallis's *Essays and Paradoxes* (1616). Initiating a movement that has gathered more and more adherents over the centuries, the writer of the anonymous piece objected to the character assassination of the last Plantagenet: 'Malicious credulity rather embraceth the partial writings of indiscreet chroniclers and witty playmakers than his laws and actions, the most innocent and impartial witnesses.' Criticism over the next two centuries was largely an *ad hoc* affair: the play might be critiqued within a Preface to one of the many editions of the complete works published in the eighteenth century during the boom period of English editing, or a critical attitude to the play might be embedded within a theatre review. Articles or lectures devoted to a systematic appraisal of *Richard III* were very rare. Something of the mid-eighteenth century's attitude can be glimpsed in Samuel Johnson's notes, in which he recognizes the play's popularity while querying its quality:

> This is one of the most celebrated of our author's performances; yet I know not whether it has not happened to him as to others to be praised most when praise is not most deserved. That this play has scenes noble in themselves and very well contrived to strike in the exhibition cannot be denied. But some parts are trifling, others shocking and some improbable.   (Johnson, 1989, p. 216)

Johnson particularly disapproved of Richard's second wooing scene, with Elizabeth, which he felt was almost beneath criticism: 'part of it is ridiculous and the whole improbable' (p. 216) – he probably assumed, as have a surprising number of critics, that Richard's wooing was successful. The implicit contrast drawn between theatrical efficacy ('striking in the exhibition') and psychological probability sounds a keynote in the history of the play's criticism.

The last quarter of the eighteenth century saw the emergence of a character-based approach to Shakespeare that would dominate English literary criticism until the dawn of the twentieth century. In 1774 William Richardson published *A Philosophical Analysis and Illustration of some of Shakespeare's remarkable Characters*, and three years later Maurice Morgann produced the ground-breaking *Essay on the Dramatic Character of Sir John Falstaff*, a tongue-in-cheek defence of the fat knight's courage. Even before these, in the late 1760s, Thomas Whately, MP, was planning an ambitious study of 'eight or ten' of Shakespeare's principal characters. In the event he wrote about two, Macbeth and Richard, before abandoning the project in order to make his *Observations on Modern Gardening*. In the second edition of *Remarks on Some of the Characters of Shakspeare*, the 'Advertisement to the Reader' claimed complete originality for the critic: 'not one of the numerous commentators upon Shakspeare's Plays having pursued the same plan' (pp. vii–viii). 'To the same length' it might have added. The comparison between the two usurping kings was becoming commonplace, but Whately was the first to examine it in such detail in an attempt to prove that 'from the beginning of their history to their last moments, are the characters of Macbeth and Richard preserved entire and distinct' (p. 89). Richard's ruling passion is 'lust of power' (p. 28), which he combines with an infallible cheerfulness, 'equal to every occasion, coolly contemplating the approaches of distant dangers' (p. 57). Painting the contrast with Macbeth with thick chiaroscuro brush strokes, Whately's Richard emerges as utterly non-neurotic and almost two-dimensional. Although employing quotation copiously to make his points, Whately's method sometimes lapses into a vague impressionism that would be punished at GCSE level: as proof of Richard's assertiveness, he pointed to 'the repetition by Richard of the same words, *off with his head!* upon three or four different occasions' (p. 71). Whately's conclusion – that 'the character of Macbeth is much more complicated than that of Richard' (p. 90) – is true if complexity is defined by displays of remorse, anguish and ambivalence. Whilst the question of Richard's complexity (or lack thereof) would be taken up again later in the play's critical history, of most interest to the generation of Romantic critics who followed in his path was Whately's emphasis on the courageous intrepidity of the crookback.

Richard among the Romantics

When George Gordon, Lord Byron, published a poem attacking the flabby and moronic Prince Regent in 1814, the Tory press sought to villainize the poetic satirist. The *Morning Post* compared Byron, so he told his friend John Murray, to a 'sort of R[ichard] III – deformed in mind and *body*'. Byron added, 'The *last* piece of information is not very new to a man who passed five years at a public school' (Marchand, p. 162). The comparison with Richard was cruel, worthy of the playground. Byron had been born with a clubbed foot; as one of his biographers, Leslie A. Marchand writes:

> [he] came into the world with a physical handicap that caused him throughout his life much bodily suffering and mental agony, and that possibly did more to shape his character than it will ever be possible to calculate. (p. 9)

Sound familiar? And yet, perhaps what was meant by the newspaper as an insult was taken as a compliment. Like many critics and artists of the Romantic era, Byron's sense of the play was heavily influenced by Kean's performance. On 19 February 1814, he wrote in his journal: 'Just returned from seeing Kean in Richard. By Jove, he is a soul! Life – nature – truth – without exaggeration or diminution . . . Richard is a man; and Kean is Richard' (Byron, 1984, p. 140). Indeed, actor and character are conflated not only with each other, but also with that other great general of the Romantic imagination, Napoleon Bonaparte. In *Detached Thoughts*, Byron recalled some of those to whom he had been compared in his bustling and notorious life. The list included Milton's Satan, Shakespeare, Bonaparte and 'Kean the Actor'. If Byron is Kean, and 'Kean is Richard', then it follows that Byron is like Richard, and that that is not an unenviable thing to be.

In an age which celebrated Shakespeare for his 'negative capability' and his gift for dramatic empathy, the Romantics empathized with Richard. None may have gone so far with Richard as Coleridge did with the Dane ('I have a smack of Hamlet myself'), but Romantic critics nevertheless identified with what they took to be the character's daring, wit and will-power. While for many this was embodied in Kean's performance, for others, Cibber's adaptation and the vulgarity of certain actors meant that the real Richard was only available to the reading critic. This was Charles Lamb's characteristic response to watching G. F. Cooke in the role in 1802. Everyone who had witnessed Cooke's exertions in the part had 'come away with the proper conviction that Richard is a very wicked man, and kills little children in their beds'. The fact that Richard is a wicked man and does order the deaths of sleeping children did not deter Lamb from reaching his main point:

> But is in fact this the impression we have in reading the Richard of Shakspeare? Do we feel any thing like the disgust, as we do at that butcher-like representation of him that passes for him on the stage? . . . Nothing but his crimes, his actions, is visible; they are prominent and staring; the murderer stands out, but where is the lofty genius, the man of vast capacity, – the profound, the witty, accomplished Richard?   (Lamb, 1978, p. 35)

While Lamb may have had a more pronounced phobia to staged Shakespeare than Hazlitt (who sometimes had his doubts), and while the two men were of different political persuasions, their critical readings of Richard's character were remarkably consonant. Even Kean's performance, was for Hazlitt, flawed compared with the 'higher conception of this character' available to the reader of the play. Like Lamb, Hazlitt wanted less of the butcher and more of the aristocrat. Quoting the lines 'I was born so high. / Our eyrie buildeth in the cedar's top, / And dallies with the wind, and scorns the sun' (I.iii.263–5), he continued:

> The idea conveyed in these lines (which are indeed omitted in the miserable medley acted for *Richard III*) is never lost sight of by Shakespeare, and should not be out of the actor's mind for a moment. The restless and sanguinary Richard is not a man striving to be great, but to be greater than he is; conscious of his strength of will, his power of intellect, his daring courage, his elevated station; and making use of these advantages to commit unheard-of crimes.   (Hazlitt, 1916, p. 188)

The description of Richard as one who is 'raised high by his birth, but higher by his genius' confirms the (Lord) Byronic inflection of Hazlitt's hero.

In general, then, Romantic criticism was concerned with the effect of character on reader and/or spectator, but an important, more holistic note was sounded by the German translator and critic A. W. Schlegel, when he wrote that all the history plays form 'one great whole. It is, as it were, an historical heroic poem in the dramatic form, of which the separate plays constitute the rhapsodies' (p. 419). In 1810, roughly a year before he read Schlegel's lectures in German, Coleridge, too, argued for the coherence of Shakespeare's history plays. Advocating that 'some man of dramatic genius' should dramatize the reigns omitted by Shakespeare to create a blockbusting depiction of 'the history of our ancient kings', Coleridge seemed to anticipate the epic cycles of later theatrical history:

> It would be a fine national custom to act such a series of dramatic histories in orderly succession every Christmas holidays, and could not but tend to counteract that mock cosmopolitism which under a positive term really implies nothing but a negation of, or indifference to, the particular love of our country.   (1969, p. 242)

The effect of such a presentation would match what Coleridge elsewhere spoke of as the 'great object' of the history plays: 'to make [Shakespeare's] countrymen more patriotic; to make Englishmen proud of being Englishmen' (1960: II, pp. 229–30). This view of Shakespeare's histories as fundamentally positive, inclusive and patriotically straightforward would prove remarkably durable.

In the following pair of case studies, we can see both how attitudes to Richard's character evolved at the turn of the nineteenth century, and how, by the mid-twentieth century, the question of history had superseded character as the focus of critical debate.

Case study 1   *Sigmund Freud and George Bernard Shaw – Bourgeois Desire vs. Punch and Judy*

On an early spring day in 1922, Franz Kafka penned the following diary entry:

1 March. *Richard III*. Impotence.   (Kafka, p. 416)

It is better to be brief than tedious, as the First Executioner reminds us (I.vi.81), and Kafka's insight certainly does not outstay its welcome. It is not clear whether there is a connection – logical or otherwise – between the play and the condition. Presumably the experience of reading one had not led to the other. What is most likely is that Kafka, in common with more and more critics and readers of the twentieth century, was looking for a psychological underpinning for Richard's behaviour. This particular translation renders the German *Ohnmacht* (literally, 'without power') as impotence, but the word need not connote sexual frustration, and could rather point to a more general sense of powerlessness. But Kafka's verdict has more than a whiff of psychoanalysis about it and perhaps it is not surprising that a few hundred miles away and six years earlier, Sigmund Freud was offering his own diagnosis of the character.

Here I want to juxtapose Freud and George Bernard Shaw on Richard. Neither wrote much on the play – a few hundred words in each case – but what each wrote represents a key approach to interpretation. And, given that both had their reasons for writing what they did, their cases are also fodder for psychoanalysis, their interpretations open to interpretation. In 'Some Character-Types Met with in Psycho-Analytic Work' (1916), Freud, as was his clinical habit, turned to literature for examples of mental imbalance. Here he was interested in individuals who will not renounce the pursuit of pleasure, will not submit to the necessity of laws or social expectations, as they feel themselves to be exceptions. For Richard, Freud argued, 'the claim to be an exception is closely bound up with and is motivated by the circumstance of congenital disadvantage' (1957, p. 313). Now, if Richard simply used his disability as an excuse to pursue pleasure in any way he liked, this would 'stifle any stirring of sympathy in the audience' and, like many critics of the play, Freud had to account for why we do feel sympathy with the character. It is all there in the opening soliloquy – when Richard lists his deformities, regardless of the tone of the actor, we take his hint and fill in the gaps: Freud hears Richard say in the subtext: 'Life owes me reparation . . . I have a right to be an exception' (p. 314). This leads Freud to his major theory:

> And now we feel that we ourselves might become like Richard, that on a small scale, indeed, we are already like him. Richard is an enormous magnification of something we find in ourselves as well. We all think we have reason to reproach Nature and our destiny for congenital and infantile disadvantages; we all demand reparation for early wounds to our narcissism, our self-love. Why did Nature not give us the golden curls of Balder, the strength of Seigfried or the lofty brow of genius or the noble profile of aristocracy? Why were we born in a middle-class home instead of in a royal palace? We could carry off beauty and distinction quite as well as any of those whom we are now obliged to envy for these qualities. (p. 315)

Freud brilliantly domesticates Richard's otherwise outlandish and monstrous qualities and desires; domesticates both in the middle-class home but also in the everyday furniture of the bourgeois ego. Like Iago, we see Cassio and think of the daily beauty in his life that makes us ugly. Every time we complain that money is wasted on the rich, or when we distrust someone with good looks, or when we resent a colleague's advancement, Richard is stirring in us. Freud has no use for Hazlitt's soaring aristocrat dallying in the cedar's top. Richard's need for reparation is a universal condition, actually less acute in the upper classes, for which Nature has a ready supply of noble profiles. The Romantics wanted Richard to be fearless, energetic, and conscious of his strength of will. Freud, as befits the age of anxiety that created him and which he anatomized, reinvents Richard in the age's image: inadequate, bitter, ego-wounded and cheated of beauty and distinction by both nature and nurture. He needs, in our own post-Freudian lingo, to talk to someone.

For George Bernard Shaw, Richard, like most of Shakespeare's characters, has little psychology to reveal in the first place. In a short sketch of 1910, 'A Dressing Room Secret', he has a costumier break the news to Iago and Lady Macbeth that they are not characters: 'I know it seems presumptuous, sir, after so many great critics have written long chapters analyzing the character of Iago: that profound, complex, enigmatic creation of our greatest dramatic poet' (Shaw, 1961, pp. 243–4). But the fact remains for Shaw that Shakespeare's characters are not psychological entities with distinct subjectivities but are first and foremost functions of the dramatic plot and singing vessels for his verse-music. This anti-psychological reading was explicitly advanced twenty years before Freud in Shaw's review of Henry Irving's Richard. Of all the versions of the Punch and Judy show, Shaw wrote, 'except for those which are quite above the head of the man in the street, Shakespear's [*sic*] Richard III is the best':

> Richard is the prince of Punches: he delights Man by provoking God, and dies unrepentant and game to the last. His incongruous conventional appendages, such as the Punch hump, the conscience, the fear of ghosts, all impart a spice of outrageousness which leaves nothing lacking to the fun of the entertainment, except the solemnity of those spectators who feel bound to take the affair as a profound and subtle historic study. (Shaw, 1932: II, p. 285)

Punch, a manifestation of the lord-of-misrule figure found in most cultures, had also occurred to Samuel Johnson as a point of comparison. Some traces, he wrote, of Richard's Vice-like qualities 'are still retained in the rustic puppet plays, in which I have seen the Devil very lustily belaboured by Punch, whom I hold to be the legitimate successor of the old Vice' (p. 216). It is hard for a puppet to have subjectivity, it can only mimic autonomy while it answers to the twitches on its strings or gloves its master's hand. As we have seen, Irving conceived Richard quite differently, as one with 'a subtle intellect, a mocking, not a trumpeting duplicity, a superb daring which needs no roar and stamp, no cheap and noisy exultation' (Irving, 1994, p. 239). One of the first things any student of literature learns is that characters 'develop': that's what they do. It therefore follows in Shaw's anti-psychological reading of the play that the actor playing

Richard ought not to develop at all. Shaw thus criticized Irving for abandoning the 'virtuoso in mischief' after the coronation scene and straining for pathetic effect. Freud found grounds for identification and therefore sympathy with Richard's wounded self-love. Shaw, conversely, saw a puppet; entertaining, yes, but utterly incapable of profundity or pathos.

We should conclude by briefly placing Freud's and Shaw's readings of *Richard III* in some personal context. Both interpretations share the belief that Richard represents something timeless and universal: for Freud, status envy; for Shaw, the anarchic impulse. Both interpreters shared a profound ambivalence towards the figure of Shakespeare. Shaw, as champion of a new generation of late nineteenth-century dramatists (including himself), saw reverence for Shakespeare's plays as an obstacle to the achievement of a socially engaged theatre. He was, therefore, playfully inclined to underestimate the political content of Shakespeare and, as in his reading of *Richard*, stress the plays' lack of psychological or social profundity and their origin in the unsophisticated world of early modern London. Freud, likewise, sought to challenge the authority of his illustrious predecessor. If his reading of Richard's complex was grounded in middle-class inadequacy, it is striking to consider that Freud could not believe that 'the untutored son of the provincial citizen in Stratford' actually wrote the plays. Freud's 'Shakespeare' is in fact Edward de Vere, seventeenth Earl of Oxford, not 'born in a middle-class home' but in 'a royal palace', and therefore a more fitting object of envy than the man from Stratford (see Freud, 1991, p. 368n). Following Shaw, a number of critics have located Richard in a non-psychological tradition of stage devices and figures. Following Freud, others have treated the character as a study in pathology. The question of the role's depths and shallows, while of decreasing interest to critics, continues to haunt actors.

Case study 2   *E. M. W. Tillyard, Jan Kott and the Nightmare of History*

Although some nineteenth-century critics (notably Schlegel and Coleridge) conceived of Shakespeare's history plays as an organic whole, sustained criticism of what we now call the 'first tetralogy' was hampered by an authorship controversy. Editorial exponents of 'disintegration' theory sought to prove that what Heminges and Condell presented as 'Shakespeare' in the First Folio was not necessarily the bard, the whole bard and nothing but the bard. But with the work of the so-called New Bibliographers, from about 1930 Shakespeare's authorship was generally accepted for Parts 2 and 3 of the *Henry VI* plays, as was his effective (if not exclusive) penning of Part 1. This repossession enabled, if not encouraged, a gradual revaluation of the history plays. Written in the context of what was supposed to be 'the war to end all wars', Sir J. A. R. Marriot's *English History in Shakespeare* (1918) discovered in the history cycle an urgent call for national unity. Increasingly, critics attended to the political significance of the histories, 'political' relating both to Shakespeare's treatment of his sources and to the extent to which the plays embodied Elizabethan social philosophy. As Harold Jenkins summarized, by the early 1930s 'it became customary to interpret Shakespeare's cycle of plays according to the pattern imposed on history by Hall: the tragic story of York and Lancaster was a consequence of Bolingbroke's crime and a warning to England of the dangers of civil strife' (Jenkins, p. 7). In *Shakespeare and the Nature of Man* (1943), for example, Theodore Spencer saw the cycle, not uncommonly, as the vast working out of a violation and restoration of natural order. These trends in criticism, exacerbated by the turmoil of the Second World War, form the contextual backdrop to the twentieth century's most influential and controversial reading of the history plays.

E. M. W. Tillyard wrote both *The Elizabethan World Picture* and *Shakespeare's History Plays* (1944) when the very idea of Britain faced extinction. When Gaunt speaks of 'This England' in *Richard II*, the country's glories have already faded into the past tense: 'This other Eden, demi-paradise . . . Is now leased out' (II.i.43, 59). Tillyard wrote in a time in which any moment might bring invasion and thus the loss, the declension into the past tense, of Britain's sovereignty and liberty. For Tillyard, *Richard III* could not stand alone: 'In spite of the eminence of Richard's character the main business of the play is to complete the national tetralogy and to display the working out of God's plan to restore England to prosperity' (p. 205). Anticipating the increased frequency of cycle stagings in the postwar period, Tillyard argued that the play was a 'confused affair' and could not 'come into its own till acted as a sequel to the other three plays and with the solemnity that we associate rather with the Dionysia at Athens and the Wagner Festival at Bayreuth than with the Shakespeare Festival at Stratford' (pp. 205–6). Like most good modernists, he was at pains to separate the artist and the artwork: 'When therefore I say that *Richard III* is a very religious play, *I want to be understood as speaking of the play and not of Shakespeare*. For the purposes of the tetralogy and most obviously for this play Shakespeare accepted the prevalent belief that God had guided England into her haven of Tudor prosperity' (p. 210; my italics). Yet, nevertheless, Tillyard was convinced that Shakespeare's 'official self' was also 'entirely sincere' (p. 214) in his belief in God's merciful overseeing of and transportation from this bloody period in English history. Richmond must have seemed, in the early 1940s, an improbable if deeply-wished-for figure: the anointed defender of England against a murderous tyrant, the leader who would guide outnumbered troops to a predetermined and just victory. No matter that in Shakespeare the tyrant was home-grown; as we have seen, Olivier, remembering back to his performance (given in the year of the publication of Tillyard's book), readily conflated Richard and Hitler.

Tillyard's reading was so influential that for effectively a generation after its publication, no scholar offered a serious challenge to it. Many critics have since taken direct issue with Tillyard's thesis. It is open to criticism on two separate fronts. First, his reading of Elizabethan society as relatively homogeneous has been attacked as over-simplified and wishful (see, e.g., Henry A. Kelly (1970), Alison Hanham (1975), Graham Holderness (1985).) Secondly, his reading of Shakespeare's plays and the distribution of the playwright's sympathies has been questioned by critics who point, for example, to Hal's rejection of Falstaff as productive of profound ambivalence rather than the confident, Tudor mythic conclusion that the new king has done the right thing. If the Tudor Myth was an historical fact, Shakespeare aggressively challenged, if not debunked it in his exploration of power and politics. But perhaps the most influential rebuttal of Tillyard never mentions him by name. In *Shakespeare Our Contemporary* (1965), the Polish critic Jan Kott began by acknowledging that 'Every historical period finds in [Shakespeare] what it is looking for and what it wants to see' (p. 5). Although Kott does not apparently apply this maxim to his own reading, it is clear that he both looked for and found a particular politico-historical message in Shakespeare's histories, and that the message found was almost the opposite of that which Tillyard had discerned twenty years before. Where Tillyard saw the progress of Providence, Kott detected the circular and inescapable workings of the Grand Mechanism. For Shakespeare, he wrote, 'history stands still. Every chapter opens and closes at the same point. In every one of the plays history turns full circle, returning to the point of departure' (p. 6). The replacement for the king, whether Fortinbras, Malcolm or Richmond, will make no difference: 'when he assumes the crown, he will be just as hated as his predecessor. He has killed enemies, now he will kill former allies. And a new pretender appears in the name of violated justice. The wheel has turned full circle' (p. 6).

Kott's existence as a Polish citizen living under Communism is often cited as a determining influence on his readings of Shakespeare. Peter Brook's preface to *Shakespeare Our Contemporary* initiates the tendency. But surely it is not simply the Soviet occupation of the country, but the longer history of Poland – 'God's Playground' as one historian's study names it – that better explains Kott's view of power in Shakespeare as an endless, cyclical struggle involving the substitution of equally corrupt and oppressive regimes. When Kott wrote, Poland was suffering under merely the last of many incursions into its borders and redefinitions of its identity. Richmond, the 'liberator', invites scepticism: such figures have been seen and found desperately wanting before. But, for all their biographical and interpretive differences, Tillyard and Kott share a fundamental belief in predetermination: in both accounts, characters are swept up in an historical storm that renders them powerless to resist. In Tillyard's optimistic version, the storm, by God's grace, abates. Kott's darker vision echoes that of the angel of history as described by Walter Benjamin:

> His face is turned toward the past. Where we perceive a chain of events, he sees one single catastrophe which keeps piling wreckage upon wreckage and hurls it in front of his feet.

The storm from Paradise that blows him past this endless repetition of carnage is 'what we call progress' (p. 249). 'History is a nightmare from which I'm trying to awake' says Joyce's Stephen Dedalus. In Tillyard, England awakes; in Kott, there is nothing outside the nightmare.

Beyond Tillyard

With the global expansion of higher education and the increased importance of research to the academic profession, the last fifty years have produced more criticism – on *Richard III* and on Shakespeare *per se* – than any comparable period before. We now enter a densely populated terrain, but some prevalent trends can be discerned amidst the steady flurry of articles and books devoted both to *Richard* and to the history plays more generally. Questions of character and history still inevitably dominate critical inquiry, but these inquiries are now refracted through the prisms of theatrical performance, feminism, psychoanalysis and new (and old) conceptions of history.

Theatre and Performance

Both A. P. Rossiter (1961) and Bernard Spivack (1958) stress how the theatricality of Richard balances, if not subverts, the play's moral superstructure. Rossiter (whose own sense of humour places him temperamentally on the side of the Vice) stresses the play's dialectical, paradoxical nature: it is a 'comic history', not the 'moral history' of Tillyard's reading (pp. 144–5). Spivack, following Shaw, warns against both naturalistic and historical approaches to the play; Richard is a stage convention and to be treated as such: 'the historical figure who ruled England dissolves into the theatrical figure who ruled the English stage' (p. 395). It is not a long stretch from this position to that of Van Lann (1978), who sees the play as obsessed with and in many ways 'about' performance, a reading anticipated by Hazlitt's suggestion that 'Richard should woo [Anne] less as a lover, but as an actor' (1916, p. 189).

The real explosion of academic interest in the play in performance has taken place in the last twenty years or so. This movement into the mainstream is starkly exemplified by comparing the attention to performance given in the introductions to Hammond's Arden edition (1981; repr. 1997) and Jowett's Oxford (2000). Hammond devotes just over eleven pages to 'Richard III in Performance', roughly one-fifth of the 54 pages spent discussing the labyrinthine textual issues of the play. Hammond writes that the introduction is 'not the place' in which to discuss film versions of the play (p. 71n). Only one page covers twentieth-century stage performances, and here Hammond's typically rigorous critical attitude dissolves into gush: 'Bill Alexander's [production] for the RSC in 1984, was wonderful: gloriously imaginative and intelligent, as was Antony Sher's brilliant realization of Richard in it' (p. 72). Jowett, in contrast, begins by acknowledging the inseparability of the play from the theatre, and his stage history (38 pages) is as detailed as the format allows. Jowett is, in effect, responding to (and furthering the cause of) a number of studies devoted to the history of the play in performance, studies motivated by the relatively recent assumption that we can learn as much about Shakespeare's plays from their effects in performance as from the historical or personal conditions in which they were created. Rather than worrying about what Richard III may have meant to Shakespeare's first audiences (or even to Shakespeare himself), theatre historians have tended to concentrate on the ways in which subsequent eras have made the play meaningful. This approach seems peculiarly appropriate for a play which, in Julie Hankey's words, has 'owed its status solely to the limelight' (p. 1). Complementing actors' own accounts of what it is to act in the play (most notably Antony Sher's Year of the King and the shorter reflections offered throughout the Players of Shakespeare series), theatre historians such as Hankey (1988), Hodgdon (1991), Colley (1992), and Day (2002) have provided valuable analyses of the range of Richards discovered through four centuries of performance.

Psychoanalysis and Feminism

Building on Freud's brief but suggestive insights into the play, many critics have sought to apply psychoanalytic models to Richard III.

Most see Richard's bodily deficiency as leading to an inferiority complex and a compensatory reaction – a reading which, put that simply, adds little to Francis Bacon's 'Of Deformity' (see Chapter 2). Norman N. Holland's summary is representative: 'He lacks that basic substratum of self-esteem or narcissism that any human being (or literary character) must have in order to function: he can neither really love nor really be loved' (p. 335). Ideas of inherent evil are anathema to psychoanalysis, so the origin of the lack must inevitably be located in the family. For Norman Rabkin, the family is both source and destination of behavioural patterns. 'Richard kills his family not because he wants to be king but because he wants to kill his family' (p. 95). Our pleasure from these crimes derives from their acting out our own 'deep intrapsychic motives' (p. 101). For Michael Neill, his relationship with his mother, 'whose loathing is displayed with admirable economy', has failed to provide Richard with a clear sense of self, so that he is required to auto-generate from scratch, as it were (p. 105). What he is left with is a series of roles and performances with no substance beneath and 'no self solid enough to be loved' (p. 124).

Misogyny is a prominent component of Richard's pathology, an attitude which fuels his charged encounters with Anne, Margaret, Elizabeth and his mother. Since the early 1980s, feminist critics have sought to read the play as expressive of early modern gender ideologies. In her influential study *Suffocating Mothers*, Janet Adelman argues that the play explores the problem of aggressive masculine ambition and the consequent extinction of the female: 'though Richard's violence is always deplored, its action is replicated in a dramatic structure that moves women from positions of power and authority to positions of utter powerlessness, and finally [in Act V] moves them offstage altogether' (p. 9). Marilyn French agrees that the play, through its dominating central character, effects 'a renunciation of women and children, but also of the "feminine" qualities they (supposedly) represent' (p. 73); French concludes that 'Shakespeare's culture was misogynistic', feared 'the annihilation of the male', and that these received values informed the gendering of *Richard III*. Jean E. Howard and Phyllis Rackin similarly see the taming and ultimate erasure of women as typical of the early history plays, in which the potently subversive qualities of Joan la Pucelle and Margaret are steadily 'demystified, and all the power of agency and transgression appropriated by the male protagonist' (p. 107).

New and Old Histories

Hugh Grady wrote, in 1991, that 'Tillyard's works have in the last twenty years suffered a reversal of fortune in influence more meteoric and startling than their original climb to pre-eminent influence' (p. 160). Many critics have followed H. A. Kelly in concluding that Shakespeare, rather than dramatizing and supporting a monolinear, providential view of English history, instead had the exceptional ability to 'unsynthesize the syntheses' of his historical sources and 'unmoralize their moralizations' (p. 304). This claim has, as Grady argues, formed the basis for a new, post-Tillyardian orthodoxy within the academy. Nevertheless, some rearguard-active critics believe the new orthodoxy overeggs the case for Shakespeare's subversiveness. Hugh Richmond – perhaps unsurprisingly for one so named – cherishes the providential reading of the play and takes issue with such critics as Rossiter, Brooke and Charnes, who, he writes, 'seem openly resentful that Richard cannot somehow be made to escape the determinism of recorded history' (1999, p. 10). R. Chris Hassell, while accepting that the play is not merely 'a mouthpiece of Tudor (or Christian) propaganda' (p. 5), nevertheless believes that most modern stage and critical interpretations have gone too far in seeking to debunk the ethical, providential framework of the play – his Richmond, far from Kott's 'new pretender', is 'attractively pious, manly, and devout', offering his prayers in 'that strong and honest Welsh accent' (p. 25). Phyllis Rackin (1990) argues that the 'ideological conflict between providential and Machiavellian notions of historical causation was built into the plays from the beginning' (p. 46), but sees the principle of historical causation in *Richard* – in contrast with that of *King John* – as fundamentally conservative and invested in the twinned notions of providence and divine right. Elsewhere, however, the post-Tillyardian consensus has continued to produce sophisticated readings. Both Marjorie Garber (1987) and Linda Charnes (1993), for example, see the play as a self-conscious meditation on the nature of historiography. For Garber, Richard's physical deformity symbolizes the playwright's own deformation of history. For Charnes, Richard, somehow conscious of the 'notorious identity' with which he begins the play, labours to seduce the audience away from this stigma. In a highly suggestive (if implicit) fusion of Freud's and Shaw's perspectives, Charnes argues that Richard is both Vice *and* 'psychologically complex': pre-cast by history as Mr Punch, his performance strives to present an 'inwardness' that would overturn the monstrous caricature offered by 'the language and signification of a hundred years of writings' (p. 68).

Critical arguments about the meaning of *Richard III* have clearly come a long way since the anonymous objection to Richard's portrait reprinted by Sir William Cornwallis in 1616. We do not know as much about the personalities and private persuasions of contemporary critics of the play as we do about, say, Byron or Freud. But recent readings have been similarly influenced by societal changes, not least the spirit of a postmodern age which increasingly distrusts notions of providential history, unified English nationalism, or, indeed, the inferiority of women. But society will change again. Like the life and deeds of the historical Richard, the meanings of Shakespeare's text will admit no absolute, definitive interpretation, only provisional degrees of probability and plausibility. The debate is, and will always be, open to newcomers.

Further Reading

The following bibliography – arranged in order of chapters – gives details of works cited whilst also offering a brief guide to some studies which may be of interest to the reader.

General

Dutton, Richard, and Jean E. Howard (eds) (2003), *A Companion to Shakespeare's Works*, vol. II: *The Histories* (Oxford: Blackwell). Readers wanting an overview of such topics as kingship, censorship, nationalism and the history play as genre should consult this excellent companion.

Moore, James A. (1986), *Richard III: An Annotated Bibliography, compiled by James A. Moore* (New York: Garland). Under eight categories (including 'Criticism', 'Editions' and 'Stage History') Moore offers synopses of almost two thousand *Richard*-related books, articles, reviews and adaptations. An essential reference point for anyone studying the play at an advanced level.

Richmond, Hugh Macrae (ed.) (1999), *Critical Essays on Shakespeare's Richard III* (New York: G. K. Hall). An ideal introduction to the play's critical history – excerpts from many of the key critics discussed in Chapter 6, ranging from Whately (1785) to Charnes (1993).

Chapter 1:   The Texts and Early Performances

Drakakis, John (ed.) (1996), *The Tragedy of King Richard the Third* (Hemel Hempstead: Harvester Wheatsheaf). An edition of Q1 that 'presents the text substantially as it was read by its first readers, replete with typographical errors'.

Gurr, Andrew (1997), 'The Shakespearean Stage', in S. Greenblatt et al. (eds), *The Norton Shakespeare* (New York and London: Norton) pp. 3281–302.

Hammond, Antony (ed.) (1997), *King Richard III* (1981; Walton-on-Thames: Thomas Nelson).

Jowett, John (ed.) (2000), *The Tragedy of King Richard III* (Oxford: Oxford University Press).

Patrick, D. L. (1936), *The Textual History of Richard III* (Oxford: Oxford University Press).

Taylor, Gray (1987), '*Richard III*', in *William Shakespeare: A Textual Companion*, ed. Stanley Wells and Gary Taylor, with John Jowett and William Montgomery (Oxford: Oxford University Press) pp. 228–63.

Urkowitz, Steven (1986), 'Reconsidering the Relationship of Quarto and Folio Texts of *Richard III*', *English Literary Renaissance*, 16 (1986) pp. 442–66. Rejects the theory that Q was the result of memorial reconstruction; recommends that we should 'read the Quarto's alternative *Richard III* along with the Folio text to delight in their dramatic variety'.

Chapter 2:   The Play's Sources and Cultural Contexts

Bacon, Francis (1996), 'Of Deformity', in *Francis Bacon: A Critical Edition of the Major Works*, ed. Brian Vickers (Oxford: Oxford University Press) pp. 426–7.

Brooks, Harold F. (1980), '*Richard III*, Unhistorical Amplifications: the Women's Scenes and Seneca', *Modern Language Review*, 75 (October 1980) pp. 721–37.

—— (1979), '*Richard III*: Antecedents of Clarence's Dream', *Shakespeare Survey* 32, pp. 145–50.

Bullough, Geoffrey (1960), *Narrative and Dramatic Sources of Shakespeare*, vol. III: *Earlier English History Plays: Henry VI, Richard III, Richard II* (London: Routledge & Kegan Paul). Includes a long extract from Hall's *Union* with shorter excerpts from *Ricardus Tertius*, *The True Tragedy of Richard III* and Seneca's *Hercules Furens*.

Jowett, John (ed.) (2000), *The Tragedy of King Richard III* (Oxford: Oxford University Press).

Kyd, Thomas (1989), *The Spanish Tragedy*, ed. J. R. Mulryne (London: A. & C. Black).

Marlowe, Christopher (1969), *The Complete Plays*, ed. J. B. Steane (Harmondsworth: Penguin).

McAlindon, T. E. (1986), *English Renaissance Tragedy* (Basingstoke: Macmillan).

More, Thomas (1976), *The History of King Richard III; and, Selections from the English and Latin Poems*, ed. Richard S. Sylvester (New Haven: Yale University Press).

Ribner, Irving (1965), *The English History Play in the Age of Shakespeare* (1957; rev. edn, Princton, NJ: Princeton University Press).

Chapter 3:   Commentary

Bloom, Harold (1998), *Shakespeare: The Invention of the Human* (New York: Riverhead Books).

Clemen, Wolfgang (1968), *A Commentary on Shakespeare's Richard III*, trans. Jean Bonheim (London: Methuen). Very thorough act/scene/line commentary – particularly good on Shakespeare's debt to, and departure from, earlier dramas.

Hammond, Antony (ed.) (1997), *King Richard III* (1981; Walton-on-Thames: Thomas Nelson).

Hankey, Julie (ed.) (1988), *Richard III*, Plays in Performance (1981; 2nd edn, Bristol: Bristol Classical Press).

Kott, Jan (1965), *Shakespeare Our Contemporary*, trans. Bolesław Taborski (London: Methuen).

Chapter 4:   Key Productions and Performances

Agate, James (1946), *The Contemporary Theatre, 1944–45* (London: George G. Harrap).

Archer, William (1971), *The Theatrical 'World' of 1896* (1897; New York: Benjamin Blom).

Bingham, Madeleine (1978), *Henry Irving and the Victorian Theatre* (London: Allen and Unwin).

Brecht, Bertolt (1987), *The Resistible Rise of Arturo Ui* (1941), trans. Ralph Manheim, in *Plays Three: Life of Galileo, The Resistible Rise of Arturo Ui, The Caucasian Chalk Circle* (London: Methuen).

Burnand, F. C. (1978), *The Rise and Fall of Richard III; or, A New Front to an Old Dicky: A Richardsonian Burlesque*, in Stanley Wells (ed.), *Nineteenth-century Shakespeare Burlesques*, vol. 4: *The Fourth Phase* (London: Diploma Press).

Burton, Hal (ed.) (1967), *Great Acting* (London: BBC).

Cibber, Colley (1889), *An Apology for the Life of Colley Cibber, Written by Himself* (1739), ed. Robert W. Lowe, 2 vols (London: John C. Nimmo).

—— (1997), *The Tragical History of King Richard III* (1699), in Sandra Clark (ed.), *Shakespeare Made Fit: Restoration Adaptations of Shakespeare* (London: J. M. Dent).

Cole, Toby and Helen Krich Chinoy (eds) (1954), *Actors on Acting: The Theories, Techniques and Practices of the Great Actors of All Times as Told in Their own Words* (New York: Crown Publishers).

Colley, Scott (1992), *Richard's Himself Again: A Stage History of Richard III* (London and New York: Greenwood Press). The best book-length stage history.

Cook, Dutton (1883), *Nights at the Play: A View of the English Stage* (London: Chatto & Windus).

Craig, Edward Gordon (1930), *Henry Irving* (London: J. M. Dent).

Day, Gillian (2002), *Shakespeare at Stratford: Richard III* (London: Arden). In her discussion of postwar RSC productions, Day usefully distinguishes between 'Political', 'Psycho-social' and 'Metatheatrical' productions.

Donaldson, Frances (1970), *The Actor-Managers* (London: Weidenfeld and Nicolson).

Downer, Alan S. (ed.) (1959), *Oxberry's 1822 Edition of King Richard III: With the Descriptive Notes Recording Edmund Kean's Performance made by James H. Hackett* (London: Society for Theatre Research).

Eyre, Richard (1990), 'On Directing *Richard III*', in Dominique Goy-Blanquet and Richard Marienstras (eds), *Le Tyran: Shakespeare contre Richard III* (Amiens: C.E.R.L.A. Amiens-Charles V) pp. 133–9.

Green, London (1984), 'Edmund Kean's Richard III', *Theatre Journal*, 36:4 (December 1984), pp. 505–24.

Hankey Julie (ed.) (1988), *Richard III*, Plays in Performance (1981; 2nd edition, Bristol: Bristol Classical Press). An excellent introductory stage history followed by an annotated text marking points of business and interpretation from a wide range of productions.

Hassel, R. Chris (1987), *Songs of Death: Performance, Interpretation, and the Text of 'Richard III'* (Lincoln, NE: University of Nebraska Press). A productive synthesis of historical, textual and performance concerns. Curiously, anti-Richard and pro-'knights in shining armor' (pp. 106–7).

Hazlitt, William (1916), *Characters of Shakespeare's Plays* (1817; Oxford: Oxford University Press).

Heilpern, John (2000), *How Good is David Mamet, Anyway? Writings on Theater and Why It Matters* (London: Routledge).

Hodgdon, Barbara (1991), *The End Crowns All: Closure and Contradiction in Shakespeare's History* (Princeton, NJ: Princeton University Press).

Hughes, Alan (1981), *Henry Irving, Shakespearean* (Cambridge: Cambridge University Press).

Irving, Henry (1994), *Theatre, Culture and Society: Essays, Addresses and Lectures*, ed. Jeffrey Richards (Keele: Ryburn Publications).

James, Henry (1949), *The Scenic Art, Notes on Acting and the Drama, 1872–1901*, ed. Allan Wade (London: Rupert Hart-Davis).

Kalson, Albert E. (1975), 'Colley Cibber Plays Richard III', *Theatre Survey*, XVI:1 (May 1975) pp. 42–55. Reprinted in Williamson and Person (eds), *Shakespearean Criticism*, vol. 14 (1991) pp. 358–63.

Lanoye, Tom and Luk Perceval (1997), *Ten Oorlog*, 3 vols (Amsterdam: Prometheus).

Loehlin, James N. (2003), ' "Top of the World, Ma": *Richard III* and Cinematic Convention', in *Shakespeare, The Movie II: Popularizing the Plays on Film, TV, Video and DVD*, ed. Richard Burt and Lynda E. Boose (London: Routledge) pp. 67–79. A very perceptive essay on the intertextuality of the Loncraine–McKellen version.

Odell, George (1963), *Shakespeare from Betterton to Irving* (1920), 2 vols (London: Constable).

Olivier, Laurence (1986), *On Acting* (London: Weidenfeld & Nicolson).

Potter, Lois (1990), 'The Actor as Regicide: Recent Versions of *Richard III* on the English Stage', in Dominique Goy-Blanquet and Richard Marienstras (eds), *Le Tyran: Shakespeare contre Richard III* (Amiens: C.E.R.L.A. Amiens-Charles V) pp. 140–50. Places the Eyre–McKellen production in context.

Rich, Frank (1998), *Hot Seat: Theater Criticism for the New York Times, 1980–1993* (New York: Random House).

Richmond, Hugh Macrae (1989), *King Richard III*, Shakespeare in Performance (Manchester: Manchester University Press).

Sainsbury, H. A. and Cecil Palmer (eds) (1939), *We Saw Him Act – A Symposium on the Art of Sir Henry Irving* (London: Hurst & Blackett).

Shaw, George Bernard (1932), *Our Theatres in the Nineties*, 3 vols (London: Constable).

—— (1961), *Shaw on Shakespeare: An Anthology of George Bernard Shaw's Writings on the Plays and Productions of Shakespeare*, ed. Edwin Wilson (New York: E. P. Dutton).

Sher, Antony (2004), *The Year of the King* (1984; revised edn, London: Nick Hern Books). One of the best books ever written on the pressures and pleasures of acting.

Stoker, Bram (1906), *Personal Reminiscences of Henry Irving*, 2 vols (London: Heinemann).

Tynan, Kenneth (1950), *He that Plays the King: A View of the Theatre* (London: Longmans).

Walkley, A. B. (1892), *Playhouse Impressions* (London: T. Unwin).

Wells, Stanley (ed.) (1997), *Shakespeare in the Theatre: An Anthology of Criticism* (Oxford: Clarendon Press).

—— (1982), 'Television Shakespeare', *Shakespeare Quarterly*, 33 (1982) pp. 261–73.

Williamson, Audrey (1948), *Old Vic Drama: A Twelve Years' Study of Plays and Players* (London: Rockliff).

Williamson, Sandra L. and James E. Person Jr (eds) (1991), *Shakespearean Criticism*, vol. 14: *Excerpts from the Criticism of William Shakespeare's Plays and Poems, from the First Published Appraisals to Current Evaluations* (Detroit: Gale Research Inc.). Reviews and theatre history essays on *Richards* from Cibber to Sher, all conveniently under one roof. Invaluable.

Chapter 5:   The Play on Screen

Ball, Robert Hamilton (1968), *Shakespeare on Silent Film: A Strange Eventful History* (London: George Allen & Unwin).

Cartelli, Thomas (2003), 'Shakespeare and the Street: Pacino's *Looking for Richard*, Bedford's *Street King*, and the common understanding', in *Shakespeare, The Movie II: Popularizing the Plays on Film, TV, Video and DVD*, ed. Richard Burt and Lynda E. Boose (London: Routledge) pp. 186–99.

McKellen, Ian (1996), *William Shakespeare's Richard III: A Screenplay Written by Ian McKellen and Richard Loncraine, Annotated and Introduced by Ian McKellen* (London: Doubleday).

Olivier, Laurence (1986), *On Acting* (London: Weidenfeld & Nicolson).

Pacino, Al (forthcoming), *Actors on Shakespeare: Richard III* (London: Faber & Faber).

Rothwell, Kenneth S. (2000), *Early Shakespeare Movies: How the Spurned Spawned Art* (Stratford-upon-Avon: International Shakespeare Association).

Sinyard, Neil (2000), 'Shakespeare meets *The Godfather*: the Postmodern Populism of Al Pacino's *Looking for Richard*', in *Shakespeare, Film and Fin de Siècle*, ed. Mark Thornton Burnett and Romona Wray (Basingstoke: Macmillan) pp. 58–72.

Willis, Susan (1991), *The BBC Shakespeare Plays: Making the Televised Canon* (Chapel Hill, NC: University of North Carolina Press).

Film and Television Versions of 'Richard III' in chronological order

Richard III, Dir. Frank Benson (1911). Perf: Frank Benson. Videocassette. Included in *Silent Shakespeare* (British Film Institute, 1999).

Richard III, Dir. James Keane (1912). Perf: Frederick Warde. Videocassette (Kino on Video, 2001).

Richard III, Dir. Laurence Olivier (1955). Perfs: Laurence Olivier, Ralph Richardson, Pamela Brown, John Gielgud. DVD (Criterion/ Voyager, 2004).

Richard III, Dir. Jane Howells. Perfs: Ron Cook, Michael Byrne, Zoë Wanamaker. Videocassette (BBC, 1983).

Looking for Richard, Dir. Al Pacino. Perfs: Al Pacino, Kevin Spacey, Alec
    Baldwin, Winona Ryder. Videocassette (Twentieth Century Fox,
    1997).
Richard III, Dir. Richard Loncraine (1995). Perfs: Ian McKellen, Jim
    Broadbent, Annette Bening. Videocassette (MGM Video/UA,
    2000).

Chapter 6:   Critical Assessments

Adelman, Janet (1992), *Suffocating Mothers: Fantasies of Maternal Origin
    in Shakespeare's Plays, Hamlet to The Tempest* (London: Routledge).
Bate, Jonathan (ed.) (1992), *The Romantics on Shakespeare*
    (Harmondsworth: Penguin).
Burden, Dennis (1985), 'Shakespeare's History Plays: 1952–1983',
    Shakespeare Survey 38 (1985) pp. 1–18. When read with Jenkins (1953),
    provides a good overview of twentieth-century criticism.
Byron, George Gordon (1984), *Lord Byron: Selected Letters and Journals*,
    ed. Peter Gunn (Harmondsworth: Penguin).
Charnes, Linda (1993). *Notorious Identities: Materializing the Subject in
    Shakespeare* (Cambridge, MA: Harvard University Press).
Clemen, Wolfgang (1968), *A Commentary on Shakespeare's Richard III*,
    trans. Jean Bonheim (London: Methuen).
Coleridge, S. T. (1960), *Samuel Taylor Coleridge, Shakespearean Criticism*,
    ed. Thomas Middleton Raynor, 2 vols (London: J. M. Dent).
—— (1969), *Coleridge on Shakespeare: A Selection of the Essays, Notes and
    Lectures of Samuel Taylor Coleridge on the Plays and Poems of Shakespeare*,
    ed. Terence Hawkes (Harmondsworth: Penguin).
Colley, Scott (1992), *Richard's Himself Again: A Stage History of Richard III*
    (London and New York: Greenwood Press).
Day, Gillian (2002), *Shakespeare at Stratford: Richard III* (London:
    Arden).
French, Marilyn (1982), *Shakespeare's Division of Experience* (London:
    Jonathan Cape).
Freud, Sigmund (1957), 'Some Character-Types Met with in Psycho-
    Analytic Work' (1916), in *The Standard Edition of the Complete
    Psychological Works*, vol. XIV, ed. James Strachey et al., 24 vols

(1953–74) (London: Hogarth Press and the Institute of Psycho-Analysis).

—— (1991), *The Interpretation of Dreams*, trans. James Strachey, Penguin Freud Library, vol. 4 (Harmondsworth: Penguin).

Garber, Marjorie (1987), 'Descanting on Deformity: Richard III and the Shape of History', in *Shakespeare's Ghost Writers: Literature as Uncanny Causality* (London: Methuen) pp. 28–51.

Grady, Hugh (1991), 'Professionalism, Nationalism, Modernism: the Case of E. M. W. Tillyard', in *The Modernist Shakespeare: Critical Texts in a Material World* pp. 158–8 (Oxford: Clarendon Press).

Hanham, Alison (1975), *Richard III and his Early Historians, 1485–1535* (Oxford: Clarendon Press). Recognizes the many distortions of the 'real' Richard perpetrated by early historians, yet argues that More's and Shakespeare's villain must have some basis in historical reality.

Hankey, Julie (ed.) (1988), *Richard III*, Plays in Performance (1981; 2nd edn, Bristol: Bristol Classical Press).

Hassel, R. Chris (1987), *Songs of Death: Performance, Interpretation, and the Text of 'Richard III'* (Lincoln, NE: University of Nebraska Press).

Hazlitt, William (1916), *Characters of Shakespeare's Plays* (1817; Oxford: Oxford University Press).

Hodgdon, Barbara (1991), *The End Crowns All: Closure and Contradiction in Shakespeare's History* (Princton, NJ: Princeton University Press).

Holderness, Graham (1985), *Shakespeare's History* (Dublin: Gill and Macmillan).

Holland, Norman N. (1966), *Shakespeare and Psychoanalysis* (New York: McGraw-Hill).

Howard, Jean E., and Phyllis Rackin (1997), *Engendering a Nation: A Feminist Account of Shakespeare's English Histories* (London and New York: Routledge).

Jenkins, Harold (1953), 'Shakespeare's History Plays: 1900–1951', *Shakespeare Survey* 6 (1953) pp. 1–15.

Johnson, Samuel (1989), *Samuel Johnson on Shakespeare*, ed. H. R. Woudhuysen (Harmondsworth: Penguin).

Kafka, Franz (1964), *Diaries, 1910–1923*, trans. Joseph Kresh, Martin Greenberg and Hannah Arendt, ed. Max Brod (Harmondsworth: Penguin).

Kelly, H. A. (1970), *Divine Providence in the England of Shakespeare's Histories* (Cambridge, MA: Harvard University Press).

Kott, Jan (1964), *Shakespeare Our Contemporary*, trans. Bolesław Taborski (London: Methuen).

Lamb, Charles (1978), *Charles Lamb on Shakespeare*, ed. Joan Coldwell (Gerrards Cross: Smythe).

Marchand, Leslie A. (1993), *Byron: A Portrait* (London: Pimlico).

Neill, Michael (1976), 'Shakespeare's Halle of Mirrors: Play, Politics, and Psychology in *Richard III*', *Shakespeare Studies*, 8 (1976) pp. 99–129.

Rabkin, Norman (1981), *Shakespeare and the Problem of Meaning* (Chicago: University of Chicago Press).

Rackin, Phyllis (1990), *Stages of History: Shakespeare's English Chronicles* (Ithaca, NY: Cornell University Press).

Ribner, Irving (1965), *The English History Play in the Age of Shakespeare* (1957; rev. edn, Princeton: Princeton University Press).

Richmond, Hugh Macrae (ed.) (1999), *Critical Essays on Shakespeare's Richard III* (New York: G. K. Hall).

Rossiter, A. P. (1961), *Angel with Horns and other Shakespeare Lectures*, ed. Graham Storey (London: Longmans Green).

Sanders, Norman (1976), 'American Criticism of Shakespeare's History Plays', *Shakespeare Studies*, 9 (1976) pp. 11–24.

Schlegel, Augustus William (1846), *A Course of Lectures on Dramatic Art and Literature*, trans. John Black (London). [*Vorlesungen über dramatische Kunst und Litteratur*, 2 vols, 1809–11]

Shaw, George Bernard (1932), *Our Theatres in the Nineties*, 3 vols (London: Constable).

—— (1961), *Shaw on Shakespeare: An Anthology of George Bernard Shaw's Writings on the Plays and Productions of Shakespeare*, ed. Edwin Wilson (New York: E. P. Dutton).

Spencer, Theodore (1943), *Shakespeare and the Nature of Man* (Cambridge: Cambridge University Press).

Spivack, Bernard (1958), *Shakespeare and the Allegory of Evil: The History of a Metaphor in Relation to his Major Villains* (New York: Columbia University Press).

Tillyard, E. M. W. (1964), *Shakespeare's History Plays* [1944] (London: Chatto & Windus).

Van Lann, Thomas F. (1978), *Role-Playing in Shakespeare* (Toronto: University of Toronto Press).

Wells, Robin Headlam, 'The Fortunes of Tillyard: Twentieth-century Critical Debate on Shakespeare's History Plays', *English Studies*, 66:5 (1985) pp. 391–403.

Whately, Thomas (1808), *Remarks on Some of the Characters of Shakspeare* (1785; 2nd edn, Oxford, 1808).

Index